LANGUAGE &
COMMUNICATION
in Primary Schools

Kate Allott and
David Waugh

Los Angeles | London | New Delhi
Singapore | Washington DC | Melbourne

Los Angeles | London | New Delhi
Singapore | Washington DC | Melbourne

SAGE Publications Ltd
1 Oliver's Yard
55 City Road
London EC1Y 1SP

SAGE Publications Inc.
2455 Teller Road
Thousand Oaks, California 91320

SAGE Publications India Pvt Ltd
B 1/I 1 Mohan Cooperative Industrial Area
Mathura Road
New Delhi 110 044

SAGE Publications Asia-Pacific Pte Ltd
3 Church Street
#10-04 Samsung Hub
Singapore 049483

© 2016 Kate Allott, David Waugh, Kirsty Anderson, John Bennett

First published 2016

Editor: Amy Thornton
Production Editor: Chris Marke
Marketing Manager: Lorna Patkai
Cover Design: Wendy Scott
Typeset by: C&M Digitals (P) Ltd, Chennai, India
Printed and bound by CPI Group (UK) Ltd,
Croydon, CR0 4YY

Library of Congress Control Number: 2016930687

British Library Cataloguing in Publication data

A catalogue record for this book is available from the British Library

ISBN 978-1-4739-4614-9
ISBN 978-1-4739-4613-2 (hbk)

At SAGE we take sustainability seriously. Most of our products are printed in the UK using FSC papers and boards. When we print overseas we ensure sustainable papers are used as measured by the PREPS grading system. We undertake an annual audit to monitor our sustainability.

LANGUAGE & COMMUNICATION
in Primary Schools

CONTENTS

ABOUT THE AUTHORS AND CONTRIBUTORS

Kate Allott

Kate is a lecturer in primary English at York St John University. She has also worked as a literacy consultant for North Yorkshire County Council, and as a regional adviser for the National Strategies Communication, Language and Literacy Development programme.

David Waugh

David is a senior teaching fellow at Durham University where he is also the subject leader for English. He has published extensively in Primary English. David is a former deputy headteacher, was Head of the Education department at University of Hull, and was Regional Adviser for ITT for the National Strategies from 2008 to 2010. As well as his educational writing, David also writes children's stories.

Kirsty Anderson

Kirsty is a former deputy headteacher and literacy consultant for the National Strategies, and is now a teaching fellow at Durham University.

John Bennett

John is a lecturer in education at the University of Hull. His main roles are in primary initial teacher education, particularly providing primary English teaching courses for postgraduate and undergraduate trainees. He previously spent 25 years working in schools as a teacher and an advisory teacher, culminating in 12 years as a primary headteacher.

Acknowledgements

We would like to thank Frances Thomas, a teacher and speech and language therapist, who read the language difficulties chapter and made such helpful comments.

We are grateful to Heather Kelly of Durham University's Biology Department for sharing her experiences of the *Biology in Schools* project and for providing case studies.

We would also like to thank Kirsty Anderson of Durham University for her chapter on addressing the needs of EAL pupils, and John Bennett of University of Hull for contributing a chapter on digital communication.

Finally, we are grateful to all the students and teachers who contributed case studies and shared their experiences.

INTRODUCTION

The history of language and communication in schools has at times seemed to be a history of periods of neglect interspersed with periods of concern and new initiatives. Attitudes to language skills have been inconsistent: on the one hand, it is recognised that these are important for children's learning in school and their success in life. Both in their working lives – interviews, meetings, working with others – and in their private lives – developing and maintaining relationships – good language skills matter. However, there is also a view that it is somehow acceptable and even charming to be inarticulate, to have difficulties speaking in public contexts, and that the highly articulate are slightly untrustworthy; 'gift of the gab' and 'silver-tongued' are not seen as entirely complimentary phrases.

Even when language and communication are seen as important, they are problematic aspects of the curriculum. Oral language is by its nature ephemeral, and therefore difficult to assess, and there is an understandable tendency to give more weight to aspects of the curriculum which are relatively straightforward to assess. There is also a difficulty in disentangling what we speak about from how we do it. If a pupil speaks fluently and confidently but conveys very little, is that effective speaking?

How do we compare that pupil with a child whose talk is concise and informative but whose style is not particularly engaging? In England, statutory end of key stage assessment in English has focused on reading and writing, with speaking and listening, the first attainment target of the 'old' National Curriculum programme of study, covered only by teacher assessment. Added to this, speaking and listening is often seen as much more difficult to manage in the classroom than paper and pencil-based tasks (Coultas, 2012). Another issue during the periods of increased focus on language and communication has been teacher subject knowledge. Early Years practitioners' understanding of early language development is often limited; some teachers do not understand distinctions between accent and dialect, or do not recognise their own non-standard usages. The changing classrooms of the twenty-first century mean that many teachers are now working with children learning English as an additional language for the first time, and are reviewing their own practice and the language environment they provide in the light of this change. Beyond these issues, there is often a lack of clarity about using language to learn and learning to use language effectively. This may seem a subtle distinction, and clearly the two may be closely linked, but it is important that the dual focus is recognised, in order that one aspect or the other is not inadvertently neglected.

A good starting point, when looking at the history of language and communication in primary schools, is The Bullock Report of 1975. Its title, *A Language for Life,* indicated its broad scope. While it covers all aspects of English, there is a remarkably strong focus on language development in the Early Years, language for learning in the middle years, and language across the curriculum. Government interest in language in schools peaked in the 1980s, and from 1987 to 1993 the *National Oracy Project* attempted to give more priority to oracy, a word invented by one of the first people to study classroom talk in this country, Andrew Wilkinson, to parallel literacy and numeracy. As part of the project a set of imaginative and well-designed training materials for teachers, the LINC materials, were produced, along with a new acronym – KAL, or knowledge about language. However, a change of government prevented the materials from ever being made available to the profession except in unofficially circulated form. The first National Curriculum (DES, 1989) made speaking and listening the first attainment target, ahead of reading and writing, and the symbolism of this was important. However, the National Literacy Strategy, introduced in 1998, again prioritised reading and writing, as its name suggested. The need to address speaking and listening was recognised as the National Strategies project grew, and detailed and useful speaking and listening materials were produced. One of the last Strategies programmes to be introduced was the *Every Child a Talker* initiative of 2008, which focused on developing early language.

Throughout the period, research into language in the classroom was continuing, increasing understanding of how talk works in schools and beginning to show evidence of the impact of high-quality classroom talk on attainment (Mercer and Dawes, 2014). In recent years Robin Alexander's (2001) major cross-cultural study comparing education in five countries led to his influential *dialogic teaching* initiative, which focused on improving language for learning. The Bercow Report (2008) and the resulting *Better Communication Research Project* focused on children with speech and language communication needs. In 2010 the government appointed Jean Gross as children's Communication Champion to identify and promote good practice. However, all these very positive developments were taking place against a background of growing concern about children's language skills, exemplified by reports such as I CAN's *The Cost to the Nation of Children's Poor Communication* (2006), and the spread of new ideas and approaches has been patchy, with implementation more difficult than might have been thought. It is in the light of this background that our book has been written.

In Chapter 1 we explore early language development, examining the ways in which children acquire language and the role of adults in this important process.

Chapter 2 examines some of the prerequisites for creating the climate for successful communication, including classroom organisation, while Chapter 3 explores the potential of talk for learning by looking at a range of subjects and the opportunities which arise when children engage in speaking and listening activities as part of their learning.

Chapter 4 explores strategies for talking with children and argues that, for both pupils and teachers, awareness of how we use language can be the first step to becoming a more skilful language user.

Chapter 5 considers the place of oral communication in the English curriculum and looks at examples of purposeful oral activities linked to literacy work.

Planning for and assessing speaking and listening is the theme for Chapter 6 as we explore effective ways of preparing for talk in the classroom.

Chapter 7 examines the communication difficulties some children face, while Chapter 8 examines some of the issues which can arise because of language variations between children and between children and teachers.

Chapter 9 addresses the needs of children for whom English is an additional language, and digital communication is the focus for Chapter 10.

We hope that this book will promote reflection on classroom practice in the light of established research and will provide ideas for future practice which incorporates a range of effective approaches to language and communication.

Kate Allott
David Waugh
March 2016

References

Alexander, R. (2001) *Culture and Pedagogy: International comparisons in primary education*. Oxford: Blackwell.

Bercow, J. (2008) *The Bercow Report: A Review of Services for Children and Young People (0-19) with Speech, Language and Communication Needs*. Nottingham: DCSF Publications.

Coultas, V. (2012) Classroom talk: Are we listening to teachers' voices? *English in Education*, 46 (2): 175–89.

DES (1975) *A Language for Life (Bullock report)*. London: HMSO

DES (1990) *English in the National Curriculum*. London: HMSO.

DCSF (2011) National Strategies *Every Child a Talker* webarchive.nationalarchives.gov.uk/.../https:/.../DCSF-00854-2008.(accessed 13.1.16)

I CAN (2006) *The Cost to the Nation of Children's Poor Communication*. London: I CAN.

Mercer, N. and Dawes, L. (2014) The study of talk between teachers and students, from the 1970s to the 2010s. *Oxford Review of Education*, 40 (4): 430–45.

Wilkinson, A. (1970) The concept of oracy. *The English Journal*, 59: 71–7.

CHAPTER 1

EARLY LANGUAGE DEVELOPMENT

Children spend many hundreds of hours in primary school learning to read and write. But by the time they start school, they have already largely mastered spoken language, a far more complex and challenging undertaking, and they do this without formal teaching and in their earliest years. It is a remarkable achievement. They learn to produce speech sounds clearly enough to be understood; they learn thousands of words; they combine those words in unlimited ways to convey meaning; and they learn to adapt their language to different situations. How do they do it? This chapter will outline children's early language development and also how it can be supported effectively in the Early Years Foundation Stage.

Theories of language development

Early behaviourist theories about how children acquire language (Skinner, 1957; Bandura, 1977) suggested that children learn to talk through imitating the language around them. Adults' positive responses encourage children to repeat what they hear, reinforcing the learning. Examples of children doing just this can be heard all the time: it can be quite unnerving for a teacher of young children to hear children playing schools and accurately reproducing the teacher's pet phrases. However, this theory does not explain children producing language they have never heard and which is not reinforced, such as the regularised verb forms which are common among three and four year olds – 'I goed', 'I wented', 'I eated'.

Chomsky's (1971) theory of a *language acquisition device* proposed a very different view from the behaviourist one. He suggested that all children are born with an innate capacity for language which allows them to make sense of the language they hear all around them, and see patterns and rules in it which they can then apply. The two views come together in the *social interactionist view* held by theorists such as Bruner (1986), who suggested that while children are active language learners, constantly working out for themselves how language works, they are supported in this by adults who provide a rich language environment and adapt their own language to meet the child's needs. Families may, for example, adopt children's own words for objects: Meg, aged two, called babies' dummies *plugs* and duvets *lids*, generalising according to the function of the objects, and the rest of the family used these words for some time. This support and encouragement begins long before children are actually talking; adults speaking to babies as if they can understand and as if their responses can be understood was considered by Murray and Trevarthen (1986) to be very important in motivating children to communicate. The desire to communicate is extremely strong in most children, and this matters because there is a huge amount to learn in order to become a skilled language user.

Strands of language development

Learning to talk involves different sets of skills and knowledge, which were described in the DfES training materials *Communicating Matters* (2005) as *strands*. This way of looking at language is useful in getting to grips with what is involved in language development, and in assessing and supporting that development. The four strands identified are:

1. Knowing and using sounds and signs (phonological development).
2. Knowing and using words (vocabulary development).
3. Structuring language (syntax).
4. Making language work (pragmatics).

The phrase 'knowing and using' can be seen as a reference to another way of looking at language – *receptive language* (what we take in and understand) and *productive language* (what we actually say). These in turn can be aligned with the Early Learning Goals for the end of the Early Years

Foundation Stage (DfE, 2014), where the goals for listening and attention and for understanding map on to receptive language, while the goal for speaking relates to productive language. The distinction can be useful as children's receptive language will always be ahead of their productive language, as is true, of course, of all language users: we all understand vocabulary and constructions which we would not be able to use successfully. We tend to be more aware of productive language, naturally, and it is important if we have concerns about a child's language to note whether these relate to productive language alone or both productive and receptive.

Parents will often describe their children as 'late talkers' or 'early talkers'. While even deciding what constitutes the milestone of a child's first word is difficult, it is true that there is wide variation in terms of the rate of children's language learning, and the age at which, for example, they begin to combine words. It is important also to note that language does not always develop uniformly across all four strands. A child may have a wide vocabulary and use complex grammatical constructions but not be able to produce a number of speech sounds, for example. However, accepting that wide variation is to be expected, it is still useful to have a picture of what can be seen when in terms of development in the four strands, in order to have some understanding of whether a child's language development is delayed in one or more strands. The following table provides an overview.

	Phonology	**Vocabulary**	**Syntax**	**Pragmatics**
6 months–2 years	Babbling includes a growing range of sounds and increasingly reflects the patterns of the language heard.	First words are recognised at around a year; production always lags behind but by 2, children may use around 100 words, although individual variation is huge.	Single words are used to convey different meanings, such as statements and requests. Word combination usually starts when children have 50–100 words.	Young babies respond to adult communication and take turns in interactions, making eye contact, smiling and vocalising. By 2, children answer simple questions.
2–4 years	Sounds are usually heard but not always produced correctly, and as a result some words are only recognisable to parents and carers, and even those close to the child will not understand everything that is said.	The rate of learning increases to about 10 words a day.	Appropriate word order begins to be used, and questions, imperatives and negatives are used. Connectives are increasingly used to express a range of meanings.	Children can start and maintain conversations. They give basic recounts of events and tell simple stories, but often crucial information is omitted or unnecessary information is included because they do not recognise the needs of the listener.

(Continued)

(Continued)

	Phonology	Vocabulary	Syntax	Pragmatics
4–6 years	Children continue to refine production of speech sounds. They can 'hear' rhymes and use vocalisations in play. A few sounds may still cause difficulties (e.g. l, s, r, v, z, ch, sh, th) and some may be ordered wrongly in words, e.g. aminal for animal, hostipal for hospital.	Vocabulary continues to increase, with more specialised words, politeness terms and the language of reasoning, e.g. might, because. Understanding of word meaning becomes deeper, e.g. multiple meanings, effect of context.	Constructions become increasingly sophisticated.	Children are able to recognise the listener's perspective and clarify misunderstandings. They modify their language to suit the social setting. Language is increasingly used in conjunction with other modes of meaning making, e.g. playing, drawing, constructing.

At four years old, on school entry, most children:

- use language which is largely correct;
- use many connectives;
- use language for many purposes;
- give connected descriptions of recent events;
- retell stories, but do not always distinguish fact from fantasy;
- ask challenging questions;
- internalise talk in play;
- talk in role;
- talk themselves through a new task;
- are learning social language (please, thank you, sorry, etc.).

Each of the four strands will now be considered in more detail.

Phonological development

Children need to be able to hear the separate sounds, or phonemes, in words, and to produce them. English is a phonologically complex language, with (depending a little on regional accents) 20 vowel phonemes, such as /aw/ and /ai/, and 24 consonant phonemes, such as /f/ and /ch/. The consonant phonemes can be combined in 49 different clusters at the beginning or end of syllables, including clusters of three such as the cluster at the beginning of 'straight'. Children take a long time to learn to produce all the English phonemes accurately in all positions in words. Their early speech is full of phonological simplifications such as 'bo' for 'ball', 'guck' for 'duck' and 'bikkit' for 'biscuit'. This can make their speech difficult to understand. Difficulties producing sounds are likely to last longer than those related to hearing, so that by the age of four there are still some sounds which children often find difficult, such as /l/, /ng/, /t/ in the middle of words such as bottle, /z/ at beginning of words, /zh/ and /ch/. Even five year olds may still pronounce /th/ as /f/ and /r/ as /w/. However, it is worth noting that some mispronunciations, and even mis-spellings of words, may be a result of mis-hearing the words, so that *windowsill* might be pronounced *windowsilve* and *beautiful* be spelled 'broowtfl'. In addition to the complexities of the sound system of English, the language also has complex and inconsistent stress patterns: consider which syllables are stressed in the word 'medicine' and which in the word 'medicinal', for example.

Vocabulary development

Children need to learn to recognise, understand and produce words and phrases. Vocabulary significantly affects language comprehension, and is one of the most significant predictors of educational success (Feinstein and Duckworth, 2006) and the variation by school starting age is huge: Waldfogel and Washbrook (2010) compared the vocabulary of children from affluent backgrounds with those from poor backgrounds, and found that the gap in vocabulary development was about 11 months, far larger than for other cognitive skills. Vocabulary development can usefully be seen as involving not only breadth – the number of words known – but also depth – clarifying and developing understanding of the meaning of words already known. Children begin to understand that some words have more than one meaning, as can be seen in the following example, where a four year old is looking at a book with an adult.

> Adult: What kind of bird is it, do you know?
> Child: No, you tell me.
> Adult: It's a robin.
> Child: A robin – that's a funny name.
> Adult: Why?
> Child: Cos my friend is called Robin, and he's not a bird!

Other words depend on context for their meaning: children need to understand that a big rabbit will be much smaller than a small elephant, for example. Children also need to develop their understanding of more abstract words such as those connected with causality and possibility; for example, at five years old they still do not understand the relative likelihood of 'possibly', 'probably' and 'definitely', and even by the age of nine only 80 per cent of children can discriminate between them successfully (Hoffner et al., 1990).

Structuring language (syntax and morphology)

Children need to be able to combine words in order to communicate more complex meanings than can be conveyed by single words. They have to learn the rules that govern how words can be combined into sentences; for example, basic word order in English is subject, verb, object (e.g. The boy ate the apple), but this is not the case in all languages. From single words children start to combine two words, often using words such as 'more' and 'no' in combination with many other words. Utterances become longer and longer, particularly once the word 'and' begins to be used, and grammatical complexity also increases, with a wider range of connectives used to express more sophisticated meanings, and increasing ability to express negatives and ask questions.

As well as developing syntax – putting words together in the right order to express ideas – children begin early on to develop an understanding of morphemes – parts of words which carry meaning. So a root word such as 'pick' can be altered in meaning by the addition of the past tense ending –ed or the prefix 'un'. Roger Brown's (1973) classic study of the language development of three children, confirmed by later studies, showed that grammatical morphemes tend to appear in the same order, with, for example, the –ing verb ending (eating, running) appearing first, at somewhere between 19 and 28 months, and the –s plural ending (apples, socks) at between 24 and 33 months. Other morphemes such as irregular verb forms (e.g. she has, he does) and contractions such as *I'm happy* and *She's eating* may not appear until around the age of four.

Pragmatics

Children need to recognise that language varies in different social situations and for different purposes, and to be able to produce language appropriate to the context. Four year olds, for example, modify their language when talking to younger children, using simpler vocabulary, shorter sentences and a higher tone. Also by the age of four, language may be used deliberately to shock. By five to seven years, the peer group becomes more important; children may alter their accent to fit in with school friends, for example. They develop more sophisticated ways of gaining attention, and begin to understand indirect commands such as 'Who can be ready first?' or 'It's a bit of a mess in here'.

Factors affecting early language development

When children arrive in nursery or the Reception class, their early experiences may have been very different. Some children will have heard huge amounts of spoken language, much of it directed at them, from birth onwards. They will have had adults making sustained efforts to communicate with them, listening and responding sensitively. They will have talked about the past and the future as well as what was going on at the time. They will have shared books, rhymes and songs, on a daily basis or even many times a day. They will have had regular opportunities to interact with other children. There will have been many shared first-hand experiences, which they will have talked about beforehand and during the experience, and which are recounted and discussed many times afterwards.

The Effective Provision of Pre-school Education (EPPE) project (Sylva et al., 2004) found that the home learning environment was more significant than socio-economic factors such as parental income, occupation and level of education in terms of children's learning. The home learning environment was described as parental involvement in activities such as reading to children, sharing songs and rhymes with children, playing with letters and numbers and visiting the library. This is a very important finding in the light of the correlation between family income and vocabulary referred to earlier: it suggests that while wealthier families are more likely to provide a good home learning environment than poorer families, the money itself is not the crucial factor but rather simple shared activities which cost nothing. Early Years practitioners have an important role in encouraging all families to provide these activities for their young children.

While it is evident that the wide variation in terms of children's language skills on school entry is affected by their experiences at home, it would be wrong to assume that schools will always offer children from less advantaged homes a better environment for language development. Two key studies in the 1980s, comparing home and school, first raised issues about the different language experiences provided by school and home, and suggested that the differences between home and school were far greater than those between different homes.

Home and school

Gordon Wells' (1985) large-scale longitudinal Bristol study suggested that even in the most disadvantaged homes the language support offered to children was better than that which they received at school. Tizard and Hughes (2002) studied four-year-old girls, half from relatively advantaged homes and half from relatively disadvantaged, who were recorded at home and nursery. They contrasted the rich, sustained conversations at home, in which children questioned, debated and reasoned, with the much more limited interactions with nursery staff. Both studies suggested a need for continuity as children moved from home to school, with schools focusing far more on the collaborative meaning-making that was such a feature of talk at home. Wells advocates more one-to-one interaction and less time in large groups as one way of achieving this. Of course, it is possible that in the 30 years since these studies were carried out there have been changes either in the home or the educational setting, or both. Wells (2009) has suggested that the increase in numbers of families with young children where both parents work outside the home might have changed the picture. Changes in Early Years practice, with a greater emphasis in many settings on child-initiated activity rather than teacher-led, may also have altered the situation.

The following transcript is an example of the kind of talk at home which Wells, and Tizard and Hughes, noted. Alex, aged three, is talking to his father about how babies are born. Emma is his younger sister.

Alex:	How did the doctors get Emma out?
Father:	Oh! Emma came out by herself; the doctors just watched. Yes.
Alex:	Why did the doctors watch?
Father:	They were just there to help if they were needed.
Alex:	How did Emma come out?
Father:	She was born out of Mummy's tummy.
Alex:	Yeah. How did be born out of she's tummy?
Father:	Well, there's a special place for babies to be born from, and that's how she was born.
Alex:	I really think she got out – got out by magic.
Father:	By magic? Yes, that's a good way to get out, isn't it?
Alex:	Did you say magic?
Father:	Mm, sort of baby magic.
Alex:	I know how to get out – they – squeeze tummies off.
Father:	Aha.
Alex:	How did they put Mummy's tummy back together?
Father:	Aha – er well it takes time; it goes back into the right shape again, doesn't it?
Alex:	But how does – no, you tell me how – er – the tummy goes back on.

Father:	Well, the tummy never comes off really. Emma just comes out of a special hole, and then the tummy gradually gets smaller and smaller. Do you remember when Mummy's tummy was big?
Alex:	Yeh. Well – well an actually Emma fitted pointing up – we fitted pointing up, the babies did actually... then by the time we was big was – was Emma anxious in Mummy's tummy?
Father:	Emma was quite small when she was born.
Alex:	Er – how – how does the – which was the special way to get Emma out?
Father:	How – how do you think Emma came out?
Alex:	Ha! Um – I – I know how Emma get – Emma came out of Mummy's toes!
Father:	Out of Mummy's toes?
Alex:	Yeah.
Father:	Yes, that's a good idea.
Alex:	Er Emma – er – I've got an idea – there – there were buttons on Mummy to get Emma out.
Father:	There's a button on Mummy?
Alex:	Yes.
Father:	Oh.
Alex:	There's a button, and then we came out. There were two buttons – there was actually there's four buttons.
Father:	Four buttons?
Alex:	Yeh.
Father:	And that lets Emma out?
Alex:	Yeh – button let Emma come out.

In this short extract from a much longer conversation, Alex plays a full part in the conversation. He talks as much as his father does: his mean length of utterance (the number of words in each turn) is 9.1 while his father's is 8.6. He chooses the topic, and we see him exploring ideas: he has several theories about how babies are born – the squeezing off of the stomach, the toes theory, the buttons theory and magic. He asks his father a number of questions – significantly more than his father asks him – and is not always satisfied with the answers he receives. He speculates and reasons, and also shows awareness of the thinking process: 'I really think...', 'I've got an idea...'. The extract exemplifies both the astounding progress that is made in language in the first years of life, and also the huge importance of adult support. Both of these themes will be returned to and developed in following chapters; the challenge for Early Years practitioners is to provide language support of this quality within their settings.

Supporting language development in the Early Years Foundation Stage

Auditing provision

The notion of communication-friendly environments has become increasingly important in recent years, as part of the response to concerns about children's language development. In comparison with many homes, Early Years settings are not the most promising of environments for supporting language: the size of the setting, the noise and bustle, the number of children, and the number of adults, who may have difficulty getting to know individual children well when they are responsible for a relatively large number of children over a relatively short time (3–5 hours a day for possibly only one school year) – all of these factors may cause difficulties. It is important therefore to review provision and ensure the setting is as communication-friendly as possible.

The national Every Child a Talker initiative (2008–2011) provided valuable audit tools for settings. It suggested that staff look for 'talking hot-spots', where children, or children and adults, seemed to engage most readily in talk. These could be places but also times in the daily routine. Did children talk most in corners of the setting or larger spaces? Did they talk most at snack time or during child-initiated activities? 'Cold-spots' were also worth noting: what places and times seemed to inhibit talk? This knowledge could then be used to enhance provision. For example, many settings began to provide dens and small, secluded corners where children seemed more confident to talk. Seating in the outdoor area – a circle of tree stumps, for example – might significantly enhance the amount of talking that took place outside. There might be more conversation at snack time if children sat around a small table at a time of their own choosing, rather than all together on the floor. The Every Child a Talker programme also advised practitioners to audit children, both as groups and as individuals, to see when and where they engaged in talk. Adult perceptions of what goes on may be very different from the reality, and it may be that some children tend to choose activities where adults are less present and sustained talk is more difficult, such as physical play outdoors, while others tend to gravitate towards adults and monopolise conversation. Since the latter are likely to be the ones who find talk rewarding, because of the rich language experience they have at home, it is possible that the children who most need language support in their early years setting are least likely to get it, unless staff recognise this and take action.

It is also useful to audit noise levels in the setting. Background noise can affect concentration and language learning, particularly for younger children and for those with some level of hearing impairment: glue ear, for example. Again, it may be that there are noisy areas (which some children may shun) and noisy times. Soft furnishings can help to reduce noise levels, and there needs to be consistent reinforcement of expectations in relation to voice levels – the 'quiet indoor voice' as opposed to the 'playground voice'.

Adult language with young children

Most adults' language is markedly different when they talk with young children. Whether consciously or not, they adapt their language to the needs of the child in a variety of ways. These include:

- using shorter utterances;
- using a restricted vocabulary, with an emphasis on words referring to common objects, actions and activities, and relatively few adjectives and adverbs;
- marking the ends of sentences by pauses;
- speaking more slowly – typically at half the speed of adult-adult talk;
- using many repetitions;
- emphasising words important to the meaning;
- using simpler syntax and morphology, with verbs usually in the present tense, and fewer conjunctions;
- focusing talk largely on the current shared context.

In the Early Years Foundation Stage, it is important that all practitioners modify their language appropriately in order to support the children's language development. This means that they do need to be conscious of making the adaptations listed above, while at the same time ensuring that they do provide challenge – for example, by introducing and teaching new vocabulary.

Purposes for talk

A communication-friendly environment is not just a physical environment: it also includes the experiences provided for children and interaction with adults. Interesting resources and activities should stimulate talk. Visits and visitors provide shared experiences which are often talked about long after the event. Children need reasons to talk, whether this is to ask for or give information, give orders, persuade, entertain. Think how persistent they can be when asking for a treat: 'pester power' shows language very much in action – or consider how acute children's hearing is when adults are talking about things the children are not supposed to know about. The following example shows a child demonstrating a huge step forward in language, in response to a real need to communicate.

Elizabeth, aged four, had significant language delay and had never used question words. When she left the nursery with a nursery nurse for a small group activity elsewhere in the school, the adult set off in a different direction as the usual room was not available.

Elizabeth: Us going a wrong way.
Adult: [who would normally have provided an explanation] Yes.
Elizabeth: [pause] Why... us going a wrong way?

When planning activities it is important, therefore, to think carefully about what opportunities for talk will be offered. Tasting different fruits, a common activity in Early Years classrooms, may be very enjoyable but asking children to think of words to describe the fruit does not seem to have any real purpose from the child's point of view. The children do not have an extensive vocabulary to help them distinguish between the taste of a mango and the taste of a kiwi fruit, and indeed many adults would find this difficult. Also, the activity does not require more than brief responses – 'nice', 'sweet', 'yummy'; compare these to Alex's conversation with his father.

Planning for language development

It is important that all children, but particularly those whose language is less well developed, participate regularly in small group activities with a focus on language. Many of these are likely to focus on narrative – for example, telling or retelling stories, perhaps using props, puppets or small world toys. Role play is also likely to involve the development of narrative. Where the role-play theme is one which the children may not be very familiar with, it is important for adults to model not only possible scenarios but also language associated with the scenario. Chapter 6 looks in more detail at planning issues.

Case study   The Talking Time project

Dockrell et al.'s *Talking Time* project (2006) addressed concerns about the oral language skills of children entering school. An observational study in 12 inner-city nurseries showed that the best language support occurred in adult-led small group activities, but that many children did not choose to participate in such activities. The project involved training staff to lead regular small group sessions with a focus on developing language through creating narratives using role play, picture books or photographs. Staff were asked to avoid asking direct questions or following an inflexible script, or making children repeat what was said. All children participated in two 15-minute group sessions a week, in small groups of four to six, with a range of language levels in each group.

The progress of children in the project was compared with a control group where there was no intervention and a group receiving a story-reading intervention. The study showed that the structured language activities did improve children's language, but they did not catch up with age-related expectations. The improved quality of adults' language with children was generalised from the Talking Time activities to all interactions, but staff perceptions about language development and the children's level of language were not altered. The research team emphasised the importance of practitioner knowledge about language development and the need to plan regular language-focused small group activities for children at risk of entering school with delayed language skills.

Supporting vocabulary development

Vocabulary is crucial to learning. The links between vocabulary and reading comprehension are well established, but children with limited vocabularies are likely to have difficulties with language comprehension generally, and where a child at home may ask about unfamiliar words, children at school will either try to work out the meaning of words they hear from the context, sometimes successfully but sometimes not, or may come to expect not to understand a proportion of what is said to them, and as a result to be less engaged with their learning. Of course, this is true of adults as well; we are often reluctant to ask about words or acronyms we do not understand, even when this interferes with our wider comprehension.

Key vocabulary is often identified in planning, but thought needs to be given to selecting the words to be taught, and the strategies for teaching. It is important first to check that the children do not already know the words. Of course, it may well be that some children do and others do not, but no teacher would want to feel that children who have developed a wide vocabulary at home do not have opportunities to continue to extend it at school. Second, the words should be considered in the light of possible future use. If a word is so specialised that it is likely only to be used in relation to a specific topic, children may not have the opportunity to consolidate their knowledge and understanding of it by using it after the topic has ended. When a book is shared with children, thought should be given to which words in it should be a focus of vocabulary development, and when. Rather than interrupt the reading of a story to explain a word, for example, it may be pre-taught (shown and discussed beforehand) or discussed afterwards, when children can use the context of the whole text to guess what the meaning may be – a useful strategy.

Strategies for teaching words should include introducing the word in a meaningful context and planning carefully how to explain it. Many definitions given spontaneously in the classroom make no sense unless one already knows the word. The word should be repeated several times when it is first introduced, and then presented, if possible in different contexts, over the next few days. Children will often need to hear a word many times before they feel confident to use it in their own language, which is the ultimate goal. Adults should model an interest in words: 'That's a funny word!' 'That's a very long word.'

Talking with young children: good practice tips

There are many simple strategies which are likely to encourage children to talk and support their language development. It is useful to film or record yourself talking with children to get a realistic picture of how effectively you do this. Often it can be a shock to realise how little talking the children do, and how all our attempts to encourage them to speak, such as asking questions, seem to have the opposite effect from the intended one. Points to remember are:

Speak clearly. Particularly where children have some level of hearing loss, it is important to enunciate words clearly. This will slow your speech down, which is also beneficial.

Talk less. The children, rather than you as a skilled language user, need opportunities to talk.

Initiating talk. Choose carefully when to try to initiate a conversation. Your well-meaning question may be an unwelcome interruption for a child who is deeply engrossed in an activity. Watch and wait before you say anything. If possible, allow the child to initiate the conversation rather than doing so yourself.

Get down to the child's level. Imagine how it must feel to have a conversation with someone twice your height. Focus on what the child is doing or looking at.

Gain attention before you begin to talk – for example, by saying the child's name.

Take turns. Be an equal partner in the talk, as you would expect to be with an adult. Both partners have the right to initiate topics and close the conversation. Do not interrupt the child's turns.

Select your starter. Avoid asking display questions to which you already know the answer, and which in any case are likely to prompt only very brief responses. Consider other initiations such as offering a comment or using starters such as 'I wonder why…?' If you are genuinely interested in what the child is doing, or what they think, it will be much easier to find something to say to get the conversation going.

Wait time. Give children time to respond. They need to process what you have said and then think about their response. Talk should be unhurried. Teach children that silence is acceptable and is often thinking time. Do not rush to fill silences; often teachers jump in while children are still formulating their thoughts.

Listen carefully to what children say. Often children are misunderstood or interesting remarks are ignored because adults are thinking more about their own part in the conversation than the child's contributions. Give yourself thinking time.

Clarify. If you do not understand what children are saying, ask them to say it again. If they repeat it and you still do not understand, ask them to show you. Some children will make every effort to get you to understand, as with Ruby who repeated 'back room keener' several times, when her teacher could not understand, and then returned to it later in the conversation, finally succeeding by replacing the phrase with 'hoover'. Other children quickly become frustrated or upset at their inability to communicate effectively.

Do not correct young children's grammar or pronunciation. It suggests that you are less interested in what they say than in how they say it, and that does not encourage communication. It is also remarkably ineffective: children will often go on saying 'I goed', 'I taked' and so on until they are ready to use the irregular but correct form. It is interesting to note that parents generally correct matters of fact but not language: for example, 'I ated it all up!' 'No, you haven't; there's lots left in your bowl.'

Use recasts of what children say in order to model correct pronunciation and grammar unobtrusively: for example, 'I splashing!' 'Yes, and I'm splashing too!'

Use expansions of what the child has said to model more complex grammar and new vocabulary: for example, 'I splashing!' 'Yes, we're both splashing in the puddle, aren't we?'

Use contrastive language to develop vocabulary: for example, 'It's muddy water, not clean water.'

Talking in sentences. Don't demand responses 'in full sentences'. In adult conversations many responses are not in grammatically complete sentences, but they give all the information that is required – indeed, often a full sentence would sound rather odd: 'Where did you put the shopping?' 'I put the shopping in the kitchen.'

Accept non-verbal responses. A shake of the head, a laugh or a shrug may communicate the child's meaning very effectively. Pushing a child to respond verbally may be counter-productive as it appears to devalue the child's non-verbal communication.

Final thoughts...

It is fascinating to observe young children's language developing, but in order to ensure the best outcomes, teachers in the Early Years need to have a good understanding of that development and of their role in supporting it, and a constant focus on language in all their interactions with children.

References

Bandura, A. (1977) *Social Learning Theory.* Englewood Cliffs, NJ: Prentice Hall.

Brown, R. (1973) *A First Language: the early stages.* London: George Allen & Unwin.

Bruner, J.S. (1986) *Actual Minds, Possible Worlds.* London: Harvard University Press.

Chomsky, N. (1971) *Syntactic Structures.* The Hague: Mouton.

DCSF (2008) *Every Child a Talker: Guidance for Early Language Lead Practitioners.* Nottingham: DCSF.

DfE (2014) *Statutory Framework for the Early Years Foundation Stage.* London: DfE.

DfES (2005) *Communicating Matters: the strands of communication and language.* Nottingham: DfES.

Dockrell, J., Stuart, M. and King, D. (2006) *'Talking Time': supporting effective practice in preschool provision.* London: Institute of Education, University of London.

Feinstein, L. and Duckworth, K. (2006) *Development in the Early Years: its signifi-cance for school performance and adult outcomes*. London: Centre for Research on the Wider Benefits of Learning, Institute of Education.

Hoffner, C., Cantor, J. and Badzinski, D.M. (1990) Children's understanding of adverbs denoting degrees of likelihood. *Journal of Child Language,* 17: 217–31.

Murray, L. and Trevarthen, C. (1986) The infant's role in mother-infant communica-tions. *Journal of Child Language,* 13: 15–29.

Skinner, B.F. (1957) *Verbal Behavior.* New York: Prentice Hall.

Sylva, K., Melhuish, E., Sammons, P., Siraj-Blatchford, I. and Taggart, B. (2004) *The Effective Provision of Pre-School Education*. Nottingham: DfES Publications.

Tizard, B. and Hughes, M. (2002) *Young Children Learning*. Oxford: Blackwell.

Waldfogel, J. and Washbrook, E. (2010) *Low Income and Early Cognitive Development in the UK*. London: Sutton Trust.

Wells, G. (1985) *The Meaning Makers: children learning language and using lan-guage to learn*. London: Hodder & Stoughton.

Wells, G. (2009) *The Meaning Makers: Learning to Talk and Talking to Learn*. Bristol: Multilingual Matters.

CHAPTER 2

CREATING THE CLIMATE FOR SUCCESSFUL COMMUNICATION

In Chapter 1 we discussed the importance of language and communication in the early years and some of the things educators can do to help facilitate talk. In this chapter, we will consider how teachers can create a 'climate' for successful communication. By *climate*, we mean both the physical environment and the atmosphere which enables communication.

In exploring this topic we will look at strategies which give structure to discussion and ground rules for talk, as well as the importance of ensuring that oral work is valued by parents and carers, colleagues and, above all, children.

Consider for a moment different situations in which you talk with friends and family. These might include being:

- at home;
- in a café or pub;
- in a car together;

- on public transport;
- in a noisy bar or club.

When you think of these situations, consider how each might support and prevent successful communication. In which situation do you feel best able to make points clearly and hear what your companions have to say? In which situations is communication difficult? And when do you have to modify what you say and how you say it?

You may have decided that you are most at ease communicating at home in a quiet room when you can make eye contact and have the freedom to move when you want to. Some pubs and cafés play music quietly in the background because it is argued that silence inhibits talk. But how does your experience change if the music is loud and it becomes difficult to hear what your companion is saying? And what about being on public transport rather than in a car? Perhaps being able to make eye contact with someone helps with communication, but is it possible to be as candid in what you say when you know that strangers might be listening?

Now consider some classrooms you've worked in. What were the factors that promoted or inhibited conversation? What could have been done to make conversation more productive? And what strategies do some teachers deliberately deploy in order to inhibit conversation?

Donoghue (2009) argues that a key factor which influences classroom listening is a *supportive classroom environment* that is relatively quiet. She maintains that children's communication develops best when they *have the chance to practice [sic] in small groups first and later in increasingly large groups* (p. 366).

Lockwood (1996) commented on classroom climate:

> If successful speaking and listening activities are to take place in the primary classroom, the right climate needs to be created from the outset. This involves the children's attitude to oracy work. Without an atmosphere of respect for oracy as a way of learning and appreciation of co-operative group work, effective speaking and listening cannot take place. (Lockwood, 1996: 7)

So what can be done to develop an attitude of respect for oracy? One strategy advocated by many researchers and used by many teachers is the creation of rules for oracy.

Ground rules for speaking and listening

Mercer and Dawes (2008) maintain that ground rules for talk reflect the need for social order in classrooms. Such rules are by no means peculiar to educational settings. Think about the situations in which you are aware of appropriate behaviours such as turn-taking, speaking through a chairperson or paying attention and responding in appropriate ways. These might include committee meetings, courtrooms, interviews, religious ceremonies and telephone conversations. Without some rules, conversation can be difficult and unproductive. As teachers, we need to establish procedures which ensure that children can interact effectively. As Smith maintains, *simply putting children into groups does not ensure that they will work as groups* (Smith, 2010: 59).

It is worth talking with children about the rules that they would like to see for discussions. As an initial language activity of the school year, children could create their own or their group's list of rules for talk, before comparing them with those created by other groups and synthesising them all into a class list. This gives children some ownership of the rules and may mean they will be more likely to obey them. A list can also provide a useful reference point when discussions break down. Teachers tend to find that when children create rules for oracy, they are very similar to the ones they might have created themselves. It is highly unlikely that rules like *Everyone should talk at once* and *No one should listen when someone is speaking* will appear!

One Year 4 class devised the following rules after paired, group and then whole-class discussions:

- always listen carefully when someone is talking;
- take turns;
- don't interrupt;
- don't argue;
- if you disagree with someone, say so politely.

This 'ownership' of oracy can be extended further where children are assigned different roles during oral lessons.

The use of roles in groups

In order to help children to assume responsibility for their own actions, they can be allocated roles within their groups. These might include:

Recorder – the person who makes an accurate written record of discussions and ensures that every person's ideas are included.

Participation checker – this person helps ensure that everyone has the chance to contribute and helps those who say little to join in.

Questioner – this person uses question words (*When? Why? Where? How? Who?*) to encourage group members to explain and elaborate on their ideas.

Noise controller – acts as a sort of chairperson to ensure noise levels stay reasonable and only one person speaks at a time. It is a good idea to discuss noise levels with children before staring discussions. Telling them 'it is too noisy' means very little, but explaining what is meant by an acceptable noise level can be more productive. For example, a teacher might say 'Only the person or people you are talking to should be able to hear what you are saying'. This provides a sort of noise meter as teachers can then say, when noise levels rise, 'I could hear what Group X were discussing even though I am on the other side of the room. What do you need to do, Group X?' Further simple guidance can be given on volume of voices, with a simple chart displayed as follows:

VOLUME OF VOICES

ONE TO ONE

Only audible to your partner

SMALL GROUP

Only audible to group members

PRESENTATION TO WHOLE CLASS

Clear voice projection so that everyone can hear.

The allocation of roles fosters positive interdependence, with an emphasis upon everyone performing a role well in order to ensure the group succeeds. It shifts responsibility to the group and away from the teacher. It also helps develop teamwork, showing children some of the ways in which adults manage discussions. You might even show children a video of a meeting taking place with a chairperson, secretary, etc. You could also show footage from *Prime Minister's Question Time* in the House of Commons, so that they can see what happens when lots of people shout at once!

Goodwin (2001: xiii) considered the prerequisites for an articulate classroom:

There are, of course, certain basic necessities, such as ensuring that children can hear each other and that the room is arranged (or easily adaptable) to be conducive to talk. But beyond the organisation of furniture, an articulate classroom is one where:

- All voices are valued

- Talk is part of the whole curriculum

- Creativity and imagination are encouraged

- Language itself is talked about.

Cremin (2009: 17–18) argues that support strategies for effective group work include:

- *Ground rules*: Create a poster with ground rules for working in groups. Highlight particular elements in different group tasks.
- *Roles for group members*: Groups decide on roles such as leader, reporter and scribe, and review these during the extended activity.
- *ARQ:* Teach the Aim, Review, Question technique to help groups monitor their progress and keep on task. Any member of the group or the teacher can play the ARQ card if they feel uncertain of where the group is heading or want to recap work so far.
- *Setting targets:* Groups decide what goals they are setting themselves and a timescale to work towards.
- *Review time:* Build in time to review the work itself, to consider how the group is operating, and for the group to set targets.

ARQ (Aim, Review, Question) is a useful technique in that it allows group members to ask the rest of the group to review what their aims are so that they can refocus on a task when discussions appear to be moving away from the topic. This can be particularly useful in maintaining on-task behaviour and gives children some ownership of the management of discussions.

Jones (1988) discussed the physical context for talk and argued that it is difficult, if not impossible, actually to have a shared conversation with upwards of 25 pupils dotted around a classroom. His solution is novel:

> To break the mould you will need to move the furniture so that everyone can hear everyone else speak and so the teacher can become part of the discussion rather than the dominant chairperson. A rule of thumb should be that anyone involved in the discussion should be able to take one step forward and punch anyone else on the nose without over-stretching. (Jones, 1988: 98)

In the following sections we will explore strategies which involve movement of children and furniture and which provide structure for oral lessons. There will, however, be no suggestions that punches might be thrown!

Circle time

Smith (2001) maintains that circle time provides opportunities for children to speak, listen and express themselves confidently within a secure environment. She sets out some simple principles:

- Everyone in the class sits in a circle. On its own, sitting in a circle gives everyone equal status and an equal voice. There is no hierarchy. Everyone has a right to speak and to be heard. To emphasise this a "talking object" is used, such as a stone or toy – children may only speak when holding the "talking object".

- Everyone has a chance to speak. No child should be interrupted when speaking, emphasising the need to listen with mutual and growing respect.

- No child is ever forced to speak; there is no pressure to contribute. If they do not want to comment children simply pass the "talking object" when it reaches them. Silence is respected.

- Names of children in the circle are never mentioned unless it is to say something good about them. The atmosphere of Circle Time is always positive about children and when difficult issues are discussed it is always in a constructive way.

- Anything discussed in the circle remains confidential. (2001: 16)

All children sit at the same level, usually on a carpet, with chairs reserved for anyone who is ill or injured. Visitors cannot sit outside the circle, and Smith relates how she even persuaded an Ofsted inspector to join the circle.

Circle time offers a structured approach to speaking and listening, and can be readily understand by children. Schools which use this technique often do so throughout the key stages and find that it can be equally successful with five year olds and eleven year olds. Co-operative learning techniques offer similar levels of structure and cater for paired, group and whole-class discussion.

Co-operative learning

Johnson and Johnson (1999) set out five basic elements that are needed for co-operative learning to be effective (see Waugh and Jolliffe, 2013: 89).

- *Positive interdependence*: students must feel that they need each other in order to complete the group's task; they 'sink or swim' together.
- *Individual accountability*: co-operative learning groups are successful only when every member has learned the material or has helped with and understood the assignment.
- *Group processing*: this involves giving students time and procedures to analyse how well their groups are functioning, and how well they are using the necessary skills. The processing helps all group members achieve while maintaining effective working relationships among members.
- *Small-group skills*: students do not necessarily come to school with the social skills they need to collaborate effectively with others; teachers need to teach the appropriate communication, decision-making and conflict-management skills to students, and provide the motivation to use these skills, in order for groups to function effectively.
- *Face-to-face interaction*: the interaction patterns and verbal exchanges that take place among students in carefully structured co-operative learning groups benefit their learning.

Advocates of co-operative learning emphasise the importance not only of structure, but also of creating a safe and supportive learning environment.

The skills of group work need to be taught and it is not sufficient simply to put children into groups and ask them to co-operate. A range of activities can be used, including at a simple level *think-pair-share,* which can be deployed to good effect during whole-class discussions. The teacher poses a question and invites everyone to think about it before sharing their ideas with a talk partner. This enables every child to be able to share ideas, including those who might be reluctant to do this in a whole class discussion.

Paired work

Kagan (2009) maintains that paired discussion enables children the security of talking with one person rather than the more daunting prospect of addressing a whole class. It allows all children to have a chance to contribute their ideas, especially when *timed pair share* is used. For example, if two children spoke for one minute each in a class discussion, the rest of the class would have been passive listeners. However, if all children were in pairs every child could speak for one minute within a two-minute period.

Some teachers worry that having half the class talking at once will be noisy and may be interpreted as showing signs of disruption should a colleague be passing by, but simple techniques can be used to regain everyone's attention, including the teacher raising an arm when it is time to stop, followed by each child who sees this doing the same until every hand is raised and the class falls silent. This approach enables children to finish sentences rather than stopping abruptly and also makes children part of the class management process. A further advantage of a timed approach is that it forces people to focus on task-related talk and does not allow drift into discussion about other topics. Paired talk can be followed by pairs coming together in fours to share ideas and pool information. A co-operative learning technique known as *snowballing* involves further combinations, with fours becoming eights and so on until the whole class shares ideas.

Sample co-operative learning strategies

There are many different co-operative learning strategies and these can be adapted for different age groups and abilities. (For further ideas, see Jolliffe, 2007.)

Paraphrasing
Members of a group listen carefully to what one person has to say about a topic and then one person is chosen to paraphrase what was said. Other members then comment on the accuracy of the paraphrasing. This might be particularly useful when linked to *jigsawing* and *envoying*.

Jigsawing

A topic might be divided up so that each group focuses on finding out about one aspect. If the topic was *birds*, for example, one group might look at migration, another at garden birds, another at food and another at birds of prey. When all the parts are put together to complete the 'jigsaw', the whole class should have greater knowledge.

Envoying

After exploring an aspect of a topic, each group sends an *envoy* to another group to provide information on what his or her group had discovered. Following the 'visit', groups could paraphrase what had been told to them for the benefit of the envoy who had been away from the group at the time. In this way every group can find out more about the whole topic and information can be pooled. *Doughnutting* provides similar opportunities.

Doughnutting

Children stand in two concentric circles of the same number, with those on the inside facing those on the outside. They share information on what they have just learned and then, at a signal from the teacher, the outside team moves a set number of places clockwise and information is shared again. This technique can also be used for story-telling where each person thinks about an event which has happened to them recently. They then tell their story to someone else. When the circle moves on, each person tells the story they have just heard, but in the first person as if the event happened to them.

Rainbowing

This strategy ensures children learn to work with a range of different people. Following small group work focused on a topic, children are given a number or colour. Those with the same number or colour join up to create groups comprising representatives of each original group. In their new group, pupils take turns to report back on their group's work and share ideas and information.

All of the above strategies demand careful planning by the teacher and consideration of the arrangement of the classroom. For example, if doughnutting is to take place, a large open space is needed, while rainbowing and envoying require space for groups to work together and, perhaps, a table for them to rest on to record information.

Classroom layout

A key consideration when planning for successful speaking and listening is the layout of the classroom. Before reading on, consider some of the classrooms in which you have worked and ask yourself the following questions:

- Did children sit in groups?
- Did they sit in rows?
- Did they sit individually?
- Did they sit in pairs?
- Was the arrangement of furniture flexible and sometimes changed?

Increasingly, tables in upper primary classes seem to be arranged in rows with children facing the board at the front of the classroom, in much the same way as can be seen in museum schools such as the one at Beamish Open Air Museum in Durham. However, many classrooms continue to be arranged in tables of four or six. Woolner et al. (2012, p. 2) assert that this classroom arrangement 'developed in response to individualized learning and child-centred approaches popular in the 1960s and 1970s, but continues to be used, with some awkwardness, in classrooms where interactive whole-class teaching is now favoured'. McNamara and Waugh argued that 'group size often seems to be determined by the furniture and its arrangement' rather than by 'educational or pedagogical considerations' (1993: 44). The key to creating a climate for talk may be to adopt a flexible approach to the arrangement of furniture and the organisation of talking groups, as can be seen in the case study below.

Case study   Changing layout to encourage productive talk

Aneela wanted her Year 6 class of 24 children to have opportunities to work together in pairs and small groups, but also needed to enable them to work independently, particularly when preparing for SATs and taking mock tests. She asked children to discuss how the classroom could be set out to enable both group and independent work. The consensus was that furniture would need to be moved according to the type of work which was to take place, but that this needed to be done quickly and easily to avoid wasting time.

Eventually, children produced diagrams of the classroom, working in maths lessons to measure and model, and various designs were displayed for everyone to study. It was agreed that one produced by Paige and Hayden would be tried for a week. This involved the 12 tables being arranged in a square around a central space, with Aneela's desk incorporated into the square. Paige and Hayden's plan for flexibility means that whenever group work was to take place only four tables (the ones in the centre of each row) need to be moved and placed with two corner tables to create four tables of six. The class found that this could be done quickly and safely because the large open space in the centre of the classroom allowed plenty of room for moving chairs and tables. The tables could also be put back into a square quickly for independent work.

Aneela discovered that there were other advantages to the arrangement, since discussion and sharing of ideas could also take place when the tables were arranged in a square. For example, she went around the room and named each child, alternately, as A or B and then asked pairs to discuss a problem or issue. She then asked all As to stay in their places and all Bs to move two places clockwise and share ideas with a different A.

She found these discussions especially productive as children were given a finite amount of time and were able to collect ideas from different people before returning to their original partners.

Of course, classrooms vary in size and shape and there are often more than 24 children in a class, so many teachers may not have the luxury of being able to adopt the kind of flexible arrangement used by Aneela. However, virtually any classroom can be adapted for different purposes and if we make adjustments to help facilitate particular oral activities we show children that these activities are valuable and sometimes warrant special arrangements being made.

There is also value in creating spaces that can be used by small groups for speaking and listening. Role-play areas are common features of early years and Key Stage 1 classrooms and can take the form of houses, kitchens, shops, restaurants, etc., but such areas are less likely to be found in Key Stage 2 classrooms. A corner of the classroom might be set up as a boardroom where groups of children could hold meetings in a formal setting. An area might be created for discussing books and other texts, with comfortable chairs or bean bags, displays of texts and a water cooler. Children can devise rules for using these areas and might work in them in small groups and in groups alongside teaching assistants.

Teaching assistants' roles

An Ofsted inspector recently told us that 'TAs can lower the grade of an observed lesson from a 1 to a 4 or raise it from a 4 to a 1'. In other words, if teaching assistants are used effectively they can be highly beneficial, but sometimes they can actually be detrimental to the quality of a lesson.

Higgins (2013) described the findings of the Sutton Trust's 'Teaching and Learning Toolkit', which evaluated evidence from more than 60 detailed summaries of educational research. The research showed that, on average, classes with TAs did not do better than those without TAs. Higgins cautioned that this did not mean that teaching assistants did not have any effect on learning, but that it was important 'to work out how support staff can best support pupils' learning as, on average, this does not happen just by them being present in the classroom or in the typical ways that schools choose to use them' (2013: 12).

If we are to use teaching assistants to manage discussion groups and to promote speaking and listening, it is important that we give clear guidance on their roles. For example, we might emphasise that they should be present to facilitate talk and sustain discussion when it begins to flag rather than to dominate discussions themselves. They might act as referees when discussions become heated or disputes arise, and they might ensure that quiet or withdrawn children have opportunities to contribute and that some children do not dominate at the expense of others. TAs can also play an invaluable role in setting up role-play areas and reflecting on how effectively they are working.

Teaching assistants can also be guided on how to ask questions which encourage discussion and make children think. As Wells and Ball in Mercer and Hodgkinson (2008, p. 173) concluded, the most important step teachers can take to promote dialogic rather than monologic talk is 'to ask questions to which there are multiple answers and then to encourage the students who wish to answer to respond to, and build upon, each other's contributions'. For both TAs and teachers, this will involve using open-ended questions to prompt discussion and keeping closed questions to which there are single answers to a minimum. While closed questions do have a function in drawing out knowledge and reminding people about factual information, as well as involving lots of children due to their brevity, they rarely prompt deeper thought and discussion.

Ensuring everyone (children, staff, parents, governors) understands the role and value of talk

One of the challenges teachers face when establishing a talking classroom is convincing parents and children of the value of working in this way. For adults whose experience of school may have been rather passive, with the teacher doing most of the talking and children spending much of their time working quietly and independently, the notion of a talking classroom may seem strange. Children too may associate talk with recreation rather than work, not feeling that they have been working hard unless they have covered lots of paper with writing or calculations, as the case study below demonstrates.

Case study   We didn't do any work today

At a parents' evening Andy, an NQT, was perturbed to hear three parents say that their children sometimes came home and in answer to the question 'What did you do at school today?' responded 'Nothing'. Andy discussed this with the parents and asked for particular instances when children had responded in this way. He identified one particular day when all three children had said this and recalled that this had been an afternoon when children had been given 'philosophical questions' to discuss in pairs and small groups. He had introduced the activity after having been on a course on philosophical discussion in the primary school. The children, he recalled, had engaged in lively discussions about questions such as:

Is it ever right to tell a lie?

Is it ever wrong to tell the truth?

Some had made notes on their discussions, but most had talked, shared ideas with partners and small groups and then taken part in a whole-class discussion. At first, children had virtually all said that it was always wrong to tell lies and that it was always right to tell the truth. However, Andy had thrown in questions to provoke discussion and this had prompted children to think more deeply. For example:

What if you have bought a surprise present for your mum or dad and they want to tidy up the cupboard where you have hidden it?

What if your gran has had a new hairdo which you think looks awful and she asks you what you think of it?

What if your friend tells you a secret and you promise to keep it and someone asks you a question which would force you to break your promise if you answered truthfully?

Following the parents' evening, Andy discussed what the parents had said with the Deputy Headteacher, Liz, who told him it was very common for children to answer 'Nothing' when asked what they had done at school, especially if lessons had not included any writing. Indeed, her own children often said the same when she discussed school with them. She suggested he draw children's attention to learning outcomes for

(Continued)

(Continued)

oral lessons and consider letting talk lead to writing, not just because this might appease parents and ensure children felt they had been working, but because it was often a natural progression. Liz gave him a copy of the *Talk for Writing* materials produced by the National Strategies in 2008 and urged him to watch some of the videos of one of the authors, Pie Corbett, working with teachers.

The case study demonstrates the importance of making it clear what you want children to achieve in oral lessons, as well as constantly emphasising the value of discussion. Sometimes it is important to remind children that through sharing ideas they are able to produce more interesting work, both orally and in writing. It can be useful to find examples of how co-operative work is part of daily life in many industries, with people working in teams to solve problems and improve productivity.

It can be helpful to ask children to produce graphic organisers and diagrams to demonstrate outcomes of discussions or findings about something they have been talking about and problems they have solved. Besides providing a useful way of recording what they have learned, this tangible outcome might also reinforce the idea that they have actually done some work and have something to show for it!

Final thoughts...

The English National Curriculum states that: 'Spoken language underpins the development of reading and writing' (DfE, 2013: 14). The Statutory Requirements for spoken language for all year groups state that:

Pupils should be taught to:

- listen and respond appropriately to adults and their peers;
- ask relevant questions to extend their understanding and knowledge;
- use relevant strategies to build their vocabulary;
- articulate and justify answers, arguments and opinions;
- give well-structured descriptions, explanations and narratives for different purposes, including for expressing feelings;
- maintain attention and participate actively in collaborative conversations, staying on topic and initiating and responding to comments;

- use spoken language to develop understanding through speculating, hypothesising, imagining and exploring ideas;
- speak audibly and fluently with an increasing command of Standard English;
- participate in discussions, presentations, performances, role play, improvisations and debates;
- gain, maintain and monitor the interest of the listener(s);
- consider and evaluate different viewpoints, attending to and building on the contributions of others;
- select and use appropriate registers for effective communication.

(DfE, 2013:18)

It is useful to reflect upon the discussions in this chapter to assess the extent to which the above requirements can be met through some of the strategies suggested.

This chapter has emphasised the importance of children being given 'ownership' of speaking and listening so that they respect each other and understand the importance of oracy as a means of sharing and acquiring knowledge and understanding. By drawing upon their ideas in devising ground rules for speaking and listening, and inviting them to suggest ways of organising the classroom for talk, we not only provide them with topics for discussion which are meaningful, but also help to create a climate for successful communication.

References

Cremin, T. (2009) *Teaching English Creatively*. London: Routledge.

DCSF (2008) *Talk for Writing*. Nottingham: DCSF.

DfE (2013) *The National Curriculum in England: Framework document*. London: DfE Publications. www.gov.uk/dfe/nationalcurriculum

Donoghue, M. (2009) *Language Arts: integrating skills for classroom teaching*. Thousand Oaks, CA: Sage.

Goodwin, P. (ed) (2001) *The Articulate Classroom: Talking and Learning in the Primary School*. London: David Fulton.

Higgins, S. (2013) What can we learn from research? in D. Waugh and S. Neaum (eds) *Beyond Early Reading*. Northwich: Critical Publishing.

Johnson, D.W. and Johnson, R.T. (1999) *Learning Together and Alone: cooperation, competitive and individualistic learning, 5th edn*. Boston, MA: Allyn & Bacon.

Jolliffe, W. (2007) *Cooperative Learning in the Classroom: putting it into practice*. London: Paul Chapman.

Jones, P. (1988) *Lipservice: the story of talk in schools*. Milton Keynes: Open University.

Kagan, S. (2009) *The Instructional Revolution*. Kagan Publishing & Professional Development. www.kaganonline.com/free_articles/dr_spencer_kagan/271/The-Instructional-Revolution,3 (accessed 13.1.16).

Lockwood, M. (1996) *Opportunities for English in the Primary School*. Stoke-on-Trent: Trentham Books.

McNamara, D. and Waugh, D. (1993) Classroom organization. *School Organization,* 13(1): 41–50.

Mercer, N. and Dawes, L. (2008) The value of exploratory talk, in N. Mercer and S. Hodgkinson (eds) *Exploring Talk in School*. London: Sage.

Smith, C. in Goodwin, P. (ed.) (2001) *The Articulate Classroom: talking and learning in the primary school*. London: David Fulton (p. xiii).

Smith, J. (2010) *Talk, Thinking and Philosophy in the Primary Classroom*. London: Learning Matters.

Waugh, D. and Jolliffe, W. (2013) *English 5–11*. London: Routledge.

Wells, G. and Ball, T. (2008) Exploratory talk and dialogic inquiry, in N. Mercer and S. Hodgkinson (eds) *Exploring Talk in School*. London: Sage Publications (pp. 167–84).

Woolner, P., McCarter, S., Wall, K. and Higgins, S. (2012). Changed learning through changed space: When can a participatory approach to the learning environment challenge preconceptions and alter practice? *Improving Schools*, 15(1): 45–60.

CHAPTER 3

TALK FOR LEARNING

Chapter 2 examined factors that help to create a climate for talk in the classroom. This chapter will explore the concept of *talk for learning*. It will examine some of the prerequisites for successful talk, which can lead to learning and concrete representations of learning across the curriculum. A series of case studies on topics in mathematics, science and current affairs will be used to exemplify good and developing practice.

Browne (2009) argued that all subjects require children to interpret and use spoken language. Teachers' explanations, descriptions, questions and evaluations require listening, answering, discussion and working out ideas through talk from children. Each subject in the curriculum has its own vocabulary and ways of using language, and words that are used in a rather general way in some subjects may have very precise meanings in others. For example, there is a very precise meaning for *perfect* when we refer to *perfect numbers* in mathematics, but we use the word *perfect* less precisely when describing *a perfect day* in a poem or song.

Browne maintains that teachers should plan to incorporate speaking and listening and collaborative work so that children have opportunities to encounter a full range of types of talk. But what do we mean by *types of talk*? Glazzard and Palmer (2015) assert that children need teachers to model and prompt the use of different 'voices' if they are to use them successfully independently. They suggest that we talk for a range of purposes including *to narrate, explain, imagine, compare, describe, evaluate, question, persuade* and *entertain*. Glazzard and Palmer go on to describe three key types of classroom talk: *exploratory, presentational* and *narrative*.

Exploratory talk

Exploratory talk takes place as we try to work out our ideas. Early Years settings include a lot of this kind of talk as children explore floating and sinking, building with bricks and so forth. They try things out and talk with others about possibilities and probabilities.

Presentational talk

Presentational talk requires us to consider an audience and might range from answering questions to formal presentations.

Narrative talk

Narrative talk involves story-telling recounting real or imaginary events. There will be a structure to the narrative, and some planning and preparation may be necessary.

A key challenge for teachers is to balance the types of talk in the classroom. If children do not have sufficient opportunities for exploratory talk, will they be less successful when asked to present their ideas or provide a narrative? One solution can be to incorporate exploratory talk into class discussions through *dialogic teaching* (see also Chapter 4). Alexander (2008) developed the concept and defined it as 'reasoned discussion', which might occur in small groups and in whole-class discussions. Talk is used to stimulate and extend thinking and understanding. Used well, dialogic teaching involves questioning to promote and extend learning. It emanates from 'Socratic questioning' in which each answer gives rise to another question. Alexander argued that interactions between teachers and pupils are often brief and involve closed questions with short answers and little opportunity for speculation and exploration. Hodson (2006) describes four conditions for effective dialogic teaching which should enable a greater use of exploratory talk:

- *collective:* pupils and teachers address learning tasks together, whether as a group or as a class, rather than in isolation;
- *reciprocal:* pupils and teachers listen to each other, share ideas and consider alternative viewpoints;
- *cumulative:* pupils and teachers build on their own and each other's ideas and chain them into coherent lines of thinking and enquiry;

- *supportive:* pupils articulate their ideas freely, without fear of embarrassment over "wrong" answers, and they help each other to reach common understandings. (Hodson, 2006: 10)

In order to illustrate how incorporating different types of talk into learning can enable children to acquire knowledge successfully and be able to present it to others, a case study from Durham University's *Biology into Schools* project is presented below.

Case study   The use of peer-to-peer learning to consolidate science knowledge

Becky's placement involved her being in school every day for a week, teaching the Y6 class topics from the human body section of the curriculum for three consecutive afternoons. The children learned about the skeleton, the heart and the teeth in well-planned lessons with plenty of engaging activities, including bone bingo, making a model skeleton and tooth headband and acting out the circulatory system. Throughout, Becky encouraged the children to learn new vocabulary by repeating and explaining the words to their friends.

On the fourth afternoon the children had to decide which activities they wanted to share with Y4 pupils and prepare any additional resources, such as posters and certificates, they needed. The children were split into groups, each group preparing an activity of their choice, with support from Becky. To produce the posters, the children had to carry out a little more research into the topics they had chosen, which helped consolidate their own understanding. They were encouraged throughout to explore their ideas together to establish common understandings. They were also encouraged to rehearse their roles in the science fair.

On the final afternoon, the Y6 children invited the Y4 children to their classroom and explained what they had been learning. Some used the posters they had made to introduce ideas to the younger children. For example, the group talking about the heart had a range of images; diagrams to show the location of the heart in the body and how blood flows through the four chambers, as well as photographs of real animal hearts. Using these as visual aids gave the Y6 children confidence in their ability to communicate their knowledge, as well as helping their young audience understand.

(Continued)

(Continued)

Becky commented that the Y6 children explained the scientific concepts involved, 'as if they had known them for a long time'. Feedback from both groups of children and their teachers was very positive and the Y4 children were keen to tell their parents what they had done in the science fair.

The success of the work in developing children's knowledge and understanding is based on some key elements in Becky's work, including:

- clear guidance on what to discuss;
- questions posed for children to explore;
- allocation of roles;
- opportunities to talk in different ways, including exploratory, presentational and narrative;
- a clear goal.

It is clear, too, that there were elements of cumulative and reciprocal talk as ideas were shared and developed, and that these elements were used by the Year 6 children when they explained concepts to Year 4.

Making use of children's prior knowledge

Myhill and Brackley (2004) argued that there were often limited opportunities created in whole class discussions to draw upon children's prior knowledge. They explored the extent to which teachers *make meaningful connections for children between their past and current learning experiences* (Myhill and Brackley, 2004: 263). They concluded that teachers needed to consider a range of pedagogical strategies which helped draw upon children's prior knowledge and that this might not always be appropriate during whole-class discussions, which might be dominated by a minority of vocal children.

Mercer asserted that learning should begin with 'enough prior shared knowledge to be able to achieve some initial joint understanding' (Mercer, 2000: 21). Mercer views the teacher as an expert guide, rather than a passive facilitator, who challenges and supports learners. Teachers achieve this by making links between prior knowledge and new learning. We should not, therefore, assume that children approach new learning completely ignorant of subject content. Indeed, they may already know aspects of what we are about to teach which will enhance the knowledge of classmates. They may also have misconceptions about topics that need to be addressed.

A simple strategy for beginning a new topic and assessing children's prior knowledge involves shared writing using pictures or artefacts. For example, as an introduction to a history topic for Key Stage 2 focusing on Romans, the teacher might download or copy a set of pictures depicting life in a Roman town. Street scenes, temples, villas, stadia, shops and so forth can be stuck to larger pieces of paper and given to pairs of children to look at. They can be asked to work together to discuss and describe what they can see and to make notes on the larger piece of paper. These can then be passed on to another pair who can review the notes and add their own. The sheets can be passed on once more and then returned to the original pairs who collate the ideas and present them as a list or a piece of prose or a diagram.

This activity enables children to share ideas, to speculate and to discuss and present. Teachers can find out what the children already know as well as their misconceptions. Questions can be posed and children can be given time to discuss them:

> *What can you see which looks familiar?*
> *What is different?*
> *What is missing from the pictures which you would expect to see in a modern town?*
> *How do you think people travelled?*
> *How do you think they told the time?*
> *How did they keep clean?*
> *What did they do for entertainment?*
> *What kind of jobs did people do?*
> *What did they eat?*

Children might also discuss and present their own questions about what they can see, and they could also pose questions for the teacher about the things they would like to find out through studying the topic. Skilful teachers can use this approach to develop dialogic teaching, which challenges and engages children and takes talk from being largely centred on answering closed questions to becoming talk for learning.

In the case study below from the *Biology into Schools* project, a student works with children on a complex topic but manages to draw upon their prior knowledge to give context and meaning to the subject matter.

Case study   Biology into Schools: communicating new and complex ideas to children

Rachel, a student on the undergraduate Biology into Schools module, was asked by the primary school where she was placed to run a lunch-time Science Club for 'Gifted and Talented' Year 5 children. Because this is a voluntary activity for the children, Rachel had complete freedom about what she taught and felt it was important to teach the children about something completely new, rather than basing her sessions on the primary science curriculum.

With this in mind, Rachel decided to teach the children something about the genetic material, DNA, over the course of five 30–40 minute sessions. She had been advised by the school, which is situated in a part of County Durham with considerable deprivation, that, though the children were the most gifted and talented within the school, they would not be regarded as exceptionally able in comparison with their peer group nationally. Bearing this in mind, Rachel thought hard about how to make complex material, normally first taught at secondary school, accessible to Year 5 children. In the session observed, she wanted to explain to them about the use of DNA fingerprinting in forensic science. Rachel made this concept accessible in a number of ways, helped by the fact that many of the children had watched television programmes where crime scenes were investigated forensically.

First, Rachel made links to the children's prior knowledge, talking about how conventional fingerprinting can be used to solve crimes. The children completed a worksheet where they took their own fingerprints and attempted to match them with pictures of different fingerprint patterns. This allowed Rachel to introduce the idea of everyone having different fingerprints and to talk about why this is the case. She explained what the word 'unique' meant and linked this to the idea of everyone having different DNA.

Rachel then moved on to talking about DNA fingerprinting and gave a simple explanation of how restriction enzymes act as DNA scissors, cutting the DNA at unique sites in each individual. She illustrated this by talking about how the same sentence, printed out, could be cut up in many different ways using a pair of scissors. Rachel then wrote a simple sentence on the whiteboard and asked children to divide it up in whichever way they chose so they could demonstrate this for themselves.

She explained very briefly how the pieces of DNA (now referred to as fragments) could be run on a gel to separate them, giving a pattern characteristic to each individual. The children had limited understanding of the specialist vocabulary here but were easily able to complete an exercise where they identified a 'criminal' from a range of suspects, by matching their DNA pattern with that found at the crime scene. The activity depended heavily on pattern recognition, which enabled the children to gain some understanding of the process without requiring specialist knowledge of gel electrophoresis.

In this case, what Rachel didn't say was as important as what she did say – it would have been easy to get diverted into a complicated explanation, but the children didn't need this to be able to understand how the patterns could be matched and the criminal found.

In the case study above, the teacher acts as an expert guide, but draws upon children's prior knowledge to help them link the familiar to the unfamiliar. This promotes discussion and enables children to learn new concepts. We might ask how this could be achieved in other subject areas. For example, how could children learn about the rain cycle, using video material and practical resources while engaging in discussion and speculation? How might they 'develop a wide range of art and design techniques in using colour, pattern, texture, line, shape, form and space' (DfE, 2013, National Curriculum for Art and Design, Key Stage 1)? These activities and many others lend themselves to productive oral work, which should help children to develop understanding.

Talk for learning in mathematics

Wood and Coltman (1998) looked at the evolution of teaching and learning styles in mathematics and maintained that in the 1940s and 1950s lessons were typically quiet and pupils were discouraged from sharing ideas: indeed, this was considered 'cheating'. Most talk came from the teacher and there was an assumption that there was a single method for tackling questions using a standard algorithm. By the 1960s and 1970s, there was considerably less didactic teaching and children typically sat in groups and worked at their own pace. Wood and Coltman assert that the later approach was 'even more catastrophic in terms of the development of a mathematical language than the previous system when at least the children listened to the teacher talking mathematics' (1998: 115). They argue that the second approach involved teachers in an administrative rather than a teaching role and offered little opportunity for children to explain their ideas or communicate mathematical thoughts.

Wood and Coltman's work appeared just as the numeracy hour was being introduced, with its mixture of didactic teaching, independent and guided work and whole-class plenary sessions. The accent in the numeracy hour, just as in the literacy hour, was on the use of correct terminology. The numeracy hour typically began with an *oral mental starter*, which was often designed to get children to solve problems without using pen and paper. The best teaching and learning in the numeracy hour occurred when children were given time to explore and discuss ideas and teachers could challenge their thinking and guide them towards understanding. However, by 2006, Mercer and Sams were arguing that children seldom worked productively in group activities, and set out to explore the role of teachers in guiding the development of children's skills in using language as a tool for reasoning.

A teaching programme called *Thinking Together* was designed to enable children to talk and reason together effectively. Mercer and Sams concluded that 'children can be enabled to use talk more effectively as a tool for reasoning; and that talk-based group activities can help the development of individuals' mathematical reasoning, understanding and problem-solving' (2006: 1). The results indicated that the teacher of mathematics played a key role in developing children's use of language for reasoning.

Through the project, children developed their ability to use language together to improve reasoning and understanding of mathematics. An interesting link was made to Alexander's work as Mercer and Sams concluded:

> Our findings also are illustrative of the value of Alexander's (2004) concept of 'dialogic teaching', as they show how judgements about the quality of the engagement between teachers and learners can be drawn from an analysis of both the structure and the pragmatic functions of teacher-student discourse. (2006: 26)

The case study below illustrates how a teacher used a practical co-operative activity to get young children to consider number sequences and place value. The focus is very much on children discussing number and arriving at conclusions together, with the teacher available to act as an expert guide when necessary.

Case study   Maths investigation: number square

Tony wanted to develop his Year 2 class's awareness of number and number values. He used playground chalk to create a large number square on the playground with numbers 1 to 100 in rows of ten:

1	2	3	4	5	6	7	8	9	10
11	12	13	14	15	16	17	18	19	20
21	22	23	24	25	26	27	28	29	30
31	32	33	34	35	36	37	38	39	40
41	42	43	44	45	46	47	48	49	50
51	52	53	54	55	56	57	58	59	60
61	62	63	64	65	66	67	68	69	70
71	72	73	74	75	76	77	78	79	80
81	82	83	84	85	86	87	88	89	90
91	92	93	94	95	96	97	98	99	100

He then worked with groups of children to familiarise them with the square. He asked them to take turns in pairs to stand on a specified square, for example 43 facing 33. He then asked them which square they thought they would be on if they made certain movements such as:

take two steps forward

take three steps to the left

move three steps back and then one to the left.

The other children were encouraged to discuss and decide where the pair would end up. Children took turns to stand on the number square in pairs and others were asked to suggest movements. Tony found that giving each pair a number square on card helped them to work out possible movements.

He was delighted to discover that the activity became a playground game for some children and noticed that they developed increasingly complex instructions for each other. Tony followed the physical movement activities with paired activities in which he asked children to imagine themselves standing on a square and then gave them movement patterns and asked them to think about and discuss where they might end up. He emphasised that it was important that children explained their reasoning to each other rather than simply focusing on getting the right answer.

Tony discussed the number square activities with colleagues, and teachers in Years 3 and 4 tried them out too, progressing to get children to move by different numbers of steps as part of learning multiplication tables.

Williams (DCSF, 2008), in a key report for the Government, maintained that the importance of engaging children in discussing mathematics was widely recognised. He asserted that discussion about number and mathematical terminology should be part of daily discourse with children. He concluded:

> Talking mathematics should not be seen simply as a rehearsal in class of the vocabulary of mathematics, novel and important though that may be for the young learner. It should extend to high-quality discussion that develops children's logic, reasoning and deduction skills, and underpins all mathematical learning activity. (DCSF, 2008: 65)

The report argued that speaking and listening skills were essential in developing mathematical understanding, and that language was a vital element as children acquired an esoteric vocabulary which they might not hear often outside school.

Making talk productive

Vygotsky (1978) argued for the importance of language as both a psychological and cultural tool. He also claimed that social involvement in problem-solving activities was a crucial factor for individual development. However, Mercer and Sams (2006: 507) noted that:

> Observational research in British primary schools has shown that the talk which takes place when children are asked to work together is often uncooperative, off-task, inequitable and ultimately unproductive.

Mercer and Sams argue that this is not surprising since the kind of talk they are asked to engage in is unfamiliar and not what they are used to in everyday life. They also maintain that teachers often do not provide sufficient guidance on how they should discuss:

> Even when the aim of talk is made explicit – 'Talk together to decide'; 'Discuss this in your groups' – there may be no real understanding of *how to* talk together or for what purpose. Children cannot be expected to bring to a task a well-developed capacity for reasoned dialogue. (Mercer and Sams, 2006: 512)

However, Mercer and Sams make it clear that 'language skills associated with improved reasoning can be effectively taught and learned' (2006: 513). They found that when children were given guidance and practice in how to use language for reasoning they were able to use language more effectively for working on maths problems together. They concluded that individual learning and understanding of mathematics could be improved when children developed their ability to use language for reasoning. Modelling by teachers can play an important role here, as teachers articulate their thinking out loud so that children can understand the processes of thinking used to solve mathematical problems.

Talk for learning in PSHCE

Personal, social, health and citizenship education may appear to be a rich area for developing discussion and dialogic teaching, given that it incorporates issues which may be of personal importance to children and about which they may hold strong opinions. This may require particular sensitivity from teachers as children discuss issues about which they may have heard extreme views outside school. There is also often a need for teachers to maintain an impartial stance, while enabling children to explore and test their ideas. This exploration is often best achieved through speaking and listening activities, sometimes allied to literacy work.

The final case study in this chapter illustrates the importance of teachers reflecting on children's response to learning activities and adapting them when they do not seem fit for purpose.

Case study   The General Election

Clare, an experienced Year 5 teacher, wanted to ensure her class knew about a forthcoming general election and understood what it involved. The school was to be closed on polling day as it was to be used as a polling station, so she felt it was doubly important that children understood why.

Clare planned a full day of work which began with children watching excerpts from news programmes and party political broadcasts. They then completed worksheets to show if they understood some of the concepts and the candidates and their parties. By break time in the morning, it was evident to Clare and her two teaching assistants that the children were generally not particularly engaged with the activities and were completing worksheets in a rather cursory manner. They decided to adopt a different approach.

Clare explained to the children, when they returned after break, that candidates for election were members of political parties and that these parties produced manifestos in which they set out their beliefs and what they would do if elected. She asked children to work in groups to invent their own political parties to stand in a class election. They could decide on

(Continued)

(Continued)

the policies they would like to put forward for the management of their class and could prepare to present these to the electorate (the rest of the class) in the afternoon. Clare showed them some examples of manifestos and leaflets that parties put through letter-boxes. She showed them another example of a political broadcast and then told the children that it was up to them to decide how to create and manage their campaign. They would also, eventually, have to select a candidate to represent their party so that the electorate could choose whom they wanted to represent them.

There was much animated discussion in the groups about policies and how to present them. Children made notes, divided up tasks, planned manifestos and speeches, and produced leaflets and posters. By mid-afternoon, they were ready to hold hustings at which their representatives presented their policies to the rest of the class. Leaflets were copied and distributed and manifestos and posters were pinned to walls so that everyone could read them. At the end of the afternoon, an election was held through a secret ballot, and children were allowed to vote for any candidate who was not a member of their party. They were encouraged to think about the policies and the way they were presented and not just to vote for someone they liked.

At the end of the day, Clare and her TAs reflected on the day and decided that it had been much more successful when children were actively involved and were able to discuss policies and their merits. They also felt that they had a better understanding of the election process than they would have gained through more individualised work using worksheets and the internet.

In the example above, the teacher and her assistants acted as facilitators and expert guides to enable children to explore and discover more about an important issue. Their ability to reflect upon a lesson which was not particularly successful and adapt it demonstrates an ability to see the potential of speaking and listening activities as a way of engaging children with their learning.

Final thoughts...

In this chapter the value of guided and supported discussion has been examined in the context of a range of subjects. The examples show how children can engage in exploratory, presentational and narrative talk and be productive and active learners. Evans (2001: 71) discussed learning about mathematics through talk and concluded:

> Unfortunately, some children are still taught mathematics in a manner which does not emphasise understanding. They can be seen working in silence on pages of meaningless sums that do not relate to real experiences in their everyday life. To be relevant, mathematics skills need to be applied to particular situations; children must be able to recognise which skills are relevant, then be able to apply them. This means that teachers need to present mathematics to young children in ways which are as near to real life situations as possible and which take into consideration the ways in which children learn.

It is worth considering Evans' words as we contemplate planning for learning in other curricular areas, and as we seek to make subjects engaging and look for ways in which children and teachers can address learning tasks together, whether as a group or as a class, rather than in isolation. It is important that they listen to each other, share ideas and consider alternative viewpoints; build on their own and each other's ideas and link them into coherent lines of thinking and enquiry; and articulate their ideas freely, without fear of embarrassment over 'wrong' answers, and help each other to reach common understandings (see Hodson, 2006, earlier in this chapter).

References

Alexander, R. (2004) *Towards Dialogic Teaching: rethinking classroom talk*. Cambridge: Dialogos.

Alexander, R.J. (2008) *Towards Dialogic Teaching: rethinking classroom talk* (4th edn). York: Dialogos.

Browne, A. (2009) *Developing Language and Literacy 3–8*. London: Sage.

DCSF (2008) *Independent Review of Mathematics Teaching in Early Years Settings and Primary Schools*: Final Report – Sir Peter Williams June 2008. London: DCSF.

DfE (2013) *The National Curriculum in England Key Stages 1 and 2 Framework Document*. London: DfE.

Evans, J. (2001) 'Five little dollies jumping on the bed' – Learning about mathematics through talk, in P. Goodwin (ed.) *The Articulate Classroom*. London: David Fulton.

Glazzard, J. and Palmer, J. (2015) *Enriching Primary English*. Northwich: Critical Publishing.

Hodson, P. (2006) Listening to children's voices: unlocking speaking and listening in the primary classroom, in D. Jones and P. Hodson (eds) *Unlocking Speaking and Listening*. London: David Fulton.

Mercer, N. (2000) *Words and Minds*. London: Routledge.

Mercer, N. and Sams, C. (2006) 'Teaching children how to use language to solve maths problems'. *Language and Education*, 20 (6): 507–28.

Myhill, D. and Brackley, M. (2004) Making connections: teachers' use of children's prior knowledge in whole class discourse. *British Journal of Educational Studies*, 52 (3): 263–75.

Vygotsky, L.S. (1978) *Mind in Society: the development of higher psychological processes*. London: Harvard University Press.

Wood, A. and Coltman, P. (1998) Talking mathematics. In: Bearne, E. ed. *Use of Language Across the Primary Curriculum*. London: Routledge, 113-26.

CHAPTER 4

TALKING WITH CHILDREN

Talk in the classroom is different from talk in other contexts. Consider, for example, the following transcript:

A: And who knows what this one is?
B: A daisy.
A: Fantastic, yes, it's a daisy. And where does it grow – in a field, in a pond, in the garden, in a vegetable plot?
C: In the garden.
A: Yes, that's right, it grows in the garden, doesn't it? And where else does it grow? Does it grow in a pond?
C: No.

(Continued)

> *(Continued)*
>
> A: No, it doesn't grow in a pond, so where else does it grow?
> D: In a field.
> A: Yes, well done, they grow in gardens and in fields. Now, who knows what this one is?

This talk is unmistakably classroom talk, with the roles of teacher and pupil obvious to anyone who has ever spent time in classrooms. If we tried to move this type of talk to another setting it would sound very odd. Consider, for example, if your next appointment with a doctor went something like this:

> Doctor: Good morning! What seems to be the problem today?
> Patient: Well, I've had a dry, tickly cough for about three weeks and it just isn't clearing up – it wakes me up at night quite a lot.
> Doctor: Well done – good answer! You described your symptoms very well.

This chapter will consider the characteristics of classroom talk, and the constraints on it, before moving on to consider effective practice: the teacher's role as a model and the effective use of questioning and feedback; children as listeners and speakers; and ways of developing discussion.

The nature of talk in the classroom

A key characteristic of classroom talk is that it is dominated by the teacher. Teacher domination of classroom talk is apparent in several ways. The old 'rule' is that about two-thirds of classroom time is taken up by talk, and about two-thirds of that talk is by the teacher (Flanders, 1970), leaving only a third to be shared among the 30 or so pupils. Teachers generally choose the topic to be talked about; they ask the vast majority of the questions; and they manage the turn-taking, deciding who is allowed to talk when. More recent research (Mroz et al., 2000) investigating the impact of the National Literacy Strategy's Literacy Hour on classroom interaction, showed much the same picture.

This may appear to be a depressing picture of talk in the classroom, bearing in mind that it is children's language, rather than teachers', which we wish to develop. There are several reasons why classroom talk is as it is. First, teachers have a managerial role, and so spend a considerable amount of time giving instructions and explanations and managing behaviour. In addition, even when the talk is focused on learning, the size of the group is a problem. It is difficult to have an orderly discussion with 25 to 30 participants, and so typically one person takes control and allocates turns, as would happen in a formal meeting where the person chairing the meeting takes this role. Also, the relationships are unequal: for a start, teachers are adults and usually know far more about most topics under discussion than the children do. This is true of parents in the home context, of course, but in the classroom, in addition, teachers are responsible for the children's learning, and this is the third reason for the unique nature of classroom talk. Unlike an informal conversation between family members or friends, where usually any participant can introduce a topic of his or her own choice, talk in the classroom has a very clear purpose: to support children's learning. Teachers therefore decide what to talk about; in the classroom time is limited and curriculum pressures are considerable, so many teachers feel they simply cannot afford to let discussion go 'off topic'. Talk is one of the most powerful ways of teaching and of assessing learning, and talking time is seen as too valuable to be wasted.

Finally, as discussed in Chapter 2, the layout of the typical primary classroom means that children often cannot see the face of other children who are talking in whole-class discussion, suggesting that whether by accident or design, all talk is mediated through the teacher. Indeed, teachers sometimes act as human megaphones, repeating inaudible contributions to discussion so that the rest of the class can hear, rather than asking – and expecting – all children to speak loudly and clearly enough to be heard by everyone.

A second key characteristic of classroom talk is the prevalence of questions, the vast majority of which are asked by teachers. Wragg and Brown (1993) recorded more than a thousand questions asked by primary school teachers: 57 per cent of them were managerial – 'Have you finished that? Who's ready now?' – while 35 per cent were questions which simply asked for recall of information, and only 8 per cent were so-called higher order questions, requiring the children to do some thinking. Interestingly, most of these were asked of individuals in one-to-one interactions rather than the whole class or a group, giving any child a very small chance of being asked a challenging question. Children ask very few questions at all, and when they do they tend to be procedural – 'Can we use rulers?' 'I've finished – what shall I do?' When teachers' questions have a learning focus rather than a managerial purpose, more often than not they already know the answer. Such questions are therefore referred to as display questions, pseudo-questions or teacher-questions. Again, there are good reasons why teachers use such questions: partly simply that they help to maintain children's attention – no one wants to be pounced on to answer a question when the mind is a million miles away from the classroom. Also it is a way of checking on children's learning: do they remember and understand what they have been taught? But heavy reliance on such questions can simply become a habit, to give an appearance of teaching and learning when really very little of either is taking place: this practice is referred to as 'recitation'. Consider this example: a teacher was fond of asking her class, 'What can't we swallow in one bite?' to which she had trained the children to reply, 'An elephant'. (Presumably this was to remind them that much learning needs revisiting and consolidation to be secure, though whether the children understood this is not known.) One day a boy burst out with 'You can't swallow the world in one bite!' and she responded, 'Don't be silly.' In effect he was being criticised for having really listened to and thought about her question. This is not to say that questions have no place in the classroom: we will consider later how questioning can be used as an effective teaching strategy, but also why it is important that children ask questions as well as answering them (which they certainly do outside school: any parent of a young child will say that this is a skill which three year olds often practise to a degree which exhausts the adult).

Another key characteristic of classroom talk is a distinctive three-part interaction known as IRF (initiation-response-feedback) or sometimes IRE (initiation-response-evaluation), first identified by Sinclair and Coulthard (1992). Typically the teacher begins with a question, a pupil offers an answer, and the teacher then gives feedback on the answer, evaluating it, and perhaps elaborating or modifying it, before moving on to the next question. Looking back to the transcript at the beginning of the chapter, we can see this pattern very clearly. While questions and answers may be characteristic of talk in other settings – an interview, for example – the evaluative feedback is not. It suggests that the teacher has a right to make a judgement on everything said by pupils. Much of the feedback is undifferentiated praise, such as 'Brilliant!' 'Fantastic!' 'Well done!' 'Superstar!' – often completely disproportionate to the achievement shown. Teachers would suggest that it is intended to boost children's self-esteem, but because such exaggerated praise is doled out so frequently it ceases to have much impact, and there is nothing left in reserve for when a child does produce a genuinely impressive response. Also, the absence of praise then becomes unsettling and children 'read' it as meaning they are wrong. A child's answer which is met with a response, such as 'Mmm,' 'Nearly, nearly,' 'Not quite,' or 'Can anyone else help?' makes it very clear that the answer was at the very least not what was expected. Indeed, even 'Interesting idea' is sometimes perceived as a negative comment, although one would hope that teachers are keen for children to have interesting ideas. Later in the chapter we will consider whether feedback on responses is always necessary and how it can be made more effective.

Case study   Analysing classroom talk

It is useful and interesting, though sometimes an uncomfortable experience, to record yourself teaching. This works best if you record yourself with the whole class or a group for 20 minutes or so, and then select a reasonably typical extract to transcribe. Transcripts can be analysed to find out, for example:

- how many speaking turns there are, and who has most;
- how many words are spoken by the different participants;
- how many questions are asked, who asks them, and what type of questions they are.

Tom, a young teacher working towards a master's degree, decided to research his own use of verbal feedback. He recorded himself teaching mathematics, English and science lessons, and noted all the verbal feedback he gave. He classified it as either general (comments such as 'well done') or specific (comments such as 'I like the way you've started your story with a question'). Tom noticed that he gave less specific feedback in mathematics lessons, where he found it difficult to go beyond whether pupils were getting the right answers or not. However, he also found that by the end of the project he was giving less praise overall but more of the specific feedback which he knew was likely to have an impact on learning, and he hypothesised that simply becoming aware of his own practice had helped him to improve it.

The role of the teacher

The case study suggests the need for teachers to recognise the importance of their own language in the classroom and how they can become more effective users and teachers of language users. The teacher's role in developing children's language skills is twofold, as the manager of talk in the classroom and as a model. Modelling means first using clear articulation and Standard English. Clear articulation has nothing to do with regional accents, and it is important to note that the National Curriculum now and in the past has made no reference to accent. However, speaking clearly is important, particularly for children learning English as an additional language and children with impaired hearing – and apart from children with a permanent impairment, winter ear infections can cause a temporary but quite significant hearing loss for many children. You can read more about Standard English in Chapter 8. Beyond these aspects, the voice is a professional tool for teachers, as it is for actors and public speakers. Teachers need to learn to vary their voice to keep children interested. This can be done by varying intonation, pitch, volume and speed, as with a musical instrument. They can switch from a whisper to a carrying voice, which reaches the back of the hall; they can emphasise key words and make dramatic use of pauses. Above all teachers need to model skilled use of language – careful, accurate and vivid word choices, construction of sentences, framing of questions and explanations, and management of productive discussion (Brien, 2012). They need to use language to structure and signpost the lesson. This may include strategies such as hooking children in with a trailer, either at the beginning of the lesson or at the end, looking towards the next lesson:

> 'In a few minutes you're going to learn some extraordinary facts about spiders.'
> 'Next time, we'll find out how people told the time before there were clocks.'

Then there is the focusing statement or question:

> 'Today our key question is: how do we know about the Romans in Britain?'
> 'The poem we're looking at today is Roger McGough's *The Fight of the Year.*'

Throughout the lesson there are likely to be verbal signposts helping children to see the structure of the session:

> 'We'll be doing three things in today's lesson...'
> 'Now we've finished our investigation, we need to move on to consider....'

Teachers also need to model 'good listening' as well as good speaking, and this will be dealt with next.

Learning to listen

Teachers place a great deal of emphasis on 'good listening'. Some young children may well be under the impression that this simply means sitting up straight with folded arms, which is much more about looking attentive than about real listening. In fact, there is a great deal to learn about listening. Of course, in conversation it is good to look interested: we all prefer our audiences to look fascinated by what we are saying, to nod and make eye contact, to laugh politely at feeble jokes, than to appear inattentive or bored. This is simply about considering the feelings of other participants in talk; talk is about social relationships as well as communication. However, much of children's listening in school happens when teachers are communicating information, instructions, explanations and so on, and the listener's role therefore involves processing a great deal of information, explanation and instruction. Many teachers are familiar with the experience of teaching a child who appears attentive but turns out not to have heard or not to have understood what was being said. Conversely, teachers are sometimes surprised to find that children whose attention has seemed to be anywhere but on the subject of the lesson are able to answer questions successfully. They may not be playing the game of looking like good listeners but inside their heads they are alert and critical processors of what they hear.

Good listening involves a range of skills. Just as reading may involve skimming, listeners may simply be monitoring fairly lightly what is being said, when they are already familiar with it, or are waiting for the crucial bits of information. Equally, when listening to something new or challenging, much more careful listening is needed, with constant self-monitoring – Do I understand this? Do I agree with it? What do I need to remember of all this? This is active listening: even when children are not responding verbally or through actions, a great deal may be happening inside their heads. But in addition to all of this, in order to become skilled listeners children need to learn to 'read' non-verbal communication as well as verbal communication: facial expression, gesture and tone of voice may reinforce messages or send contradictory ones.

Teachers need to model active listening. Too often when a child says something, the teacher's mind is already moving on to the next question or half distracted by what others in the class are doing. It is important to look interested – and also to *be* interested. If we take time to listen carefully, we will hear fascinating ideas and insights into children's views of the world every day. We will also gain valuable understanding of children's learning, including gaps and misconceptions. It may seem difficult to give real time and attention to what children are saying when there is so much to fit in to the busy school day and when the needs of the rest of the class also have to be considered, but it is essential to establish an ethos of respectful and careful consideration of everyone's contributions to talk, and we can only do this by modelling it.

Explanations

Pupils have identified the ability to give good explanations as a key characteristic of good teachers (Wragg and Brown, 2001a), but while a great deal of attention has been given to questioning as a professional skill, there has been relatively little focus on explanations. Yet teachers give explanations all the time: what words mean, why and how things happen, how processes work. A good explanation illuminates and clarifies; a poor explanation may leave children as confused or more confused, and may lead to misconceptions. Of course, non-verbal explanations may work better than any words can do: a model of the solar system, for example, or a photograph of a geographical feature, or a demonstration of how to play a musical instrument. However, these are usually accompanied by a verbal commentary in order to ensure full understanding, and many things cannot be explained except through language. Consider, for example, how you would give explanations of the meaning of the words 'spiral' and 'honour'. It would be odd to try to define 'spiral' without using a hand movement; it would be impossible to define 'honour' in any way except through words. Teachers' language skills, therefore, are crucial to this important aspect of teaching.

It is worth planning explanations in advance when possible: for example, definitions of key terminology and effective ways of explaining such as the use of analogy and examples. They need to have regard to children's prior knowledge and possible misconceptions. Careful language choices are essential: for example, in discussing how Christians celebrate Easter it is not appropriate to use 'we', which may suggest that the speaker assumes all children in the class are practising Christians, or even 'Christians', which assumes that all Christians everywhere celebrate their religious festivals in the same way. 'Most Christians' or 'many Christians' might be better choices. Vocabulary choices need to be carefully considered: if explanations contain words the children do not understand they are unlikely to be effective. School dictionaries are often very good at providing clear definitions using simple language, and when the need for an explanation or definition arises during the course of a lesson, asking children to look the word up is an effective strategy; not only will the definition probably be better than anything a teacher could produce on the spot, but also it helps to establish the dictionary habit in children. Try to produce a quick definition of the word 'symbol'. Now compare your definition with the following:

> A symbol is a shape, design or idea that is used to represent something e.g. *Huey Newton was an important symbol of black militancy.* (Collins School Dictionary, 1989)

> Something that is used to suggest or represent something else. *A dove is a symbol of peace. / The symbol for addition is +.* (Ginn Junior School Dictionary, 1997)

It is apparent that giving a definition of something abstract is difficult: children expecting a shape, design or idea might be confused by an example of a person, and might also be unfamiliar with the term 'black militancy'. The second definition is vague but the examples would probably quickly clarify the meaning.

Instructions

Giving good instructions is another professional language skill. Oral instructions will often accompany demonstration, and showing rather than telling is in many cases a preferred option, but teachers will regularly find themselves giving instructions, and may almost as regularly find themselves repeating those instructions at least once, or having to clarify them. Preparation is important: being absolutely clear about what you want the children to do is a good start. Beyond that, it is often worth explaining that the instructions will only be given once so everyone will need to listen carefully. Some children are so used to being able to ask for the instructions to be repeated, perhaps by a teaching assistant who works with them regularly, that it hardly seems worth their while to listen first time round. It is also a good strategy to say that after the instructions have been given, one pupil will be asked to repeat them as a check.

But for some children, following a series of instructions that have all been given at once, and perhaps not even in chronological order ('But before you do that, don't forget to...') is challenging. It is best if there are several steps to break the instruction giving into sections ('When you've carried out those three steps I'll explain what to do next'). For younger children, negatives cause particular confusion ('Could everyone who hasn't finished put their books in the box') and should be avoided wherever possible.

Questions

Since questions are such a significant feature of talk in the classroom, it is important that they are used to move learning forward rather than simply to manage behaviour or allow children to display what they have already learned. Questions have been categorised in different ways over time: probably the most common has been the division of questions into open and closed questions, with the implication that open questions are always 'better' in some way than closed questions. In this view, closed questions are ones which generate short answers, probably a word or two, and which have only one or a very small number of acceptable answers. Open questions, on the other hand, are likely to generate a wide range of responses and these may be more extended. Smith et al. (2004) discovered that in more than one in three of the lessons they observed, no open questions at all were asked, while highly effective teachers asked significantly more open questions than other teachers. Considering the following questions, it is easy to see which are closed and which are open:

> What time is the clock face showing?
> Why did the Romans come to Britain?
> What are the advantages of living in a city?
> Who wrote *Wuthering Heights*?

Others, however, are less clear-cut:

> How do you think Cinderella felt when the Ugly Sisters went off to the ball?
> Which was your favourite part of the book?

The question about characters' feelings, a favourite in English lessons, often produces very limited responses – sad, jealous, cross – and indeed although it is often claimed as an open question, in practice only a small number of responses would probably be considered appropriate:

> Sad (because she wanted to go to the ball).
> Angry (because the sisters and her stepmother had been mean to her).

The following would not be appropriate:

> Happy to have the chance of a quiet night in with a good book.
> Relieved that she wasn't going to the ball since she didn't have anything to wear.

The 'favourite part' question is more genuinely open in nature, but responses are often disappointing as children find it so difficult to articulate why they liked particular parts beyond describing them as funny or exciting. Perhaps, therefore, as Wragg and Brown (2001b) suggest, rather than thinking of questions as open or closed, higher order or lower order, we can only really judge them in terms of the responses they prompt: a good question is one which does what the teacher intended it to do. Indeed, it may be wrong to try to analyse single questions: very often a series of questions is needed to help children develop a line of thinking and go beyond the superficial, or to probe their understanding fully, although Wragg and Brown discovered that very few questions were used in a sequence of more than four. Often a relatively simple question acts as a starter to focus children, and can then be followed up by a much more challenging question:

> Who's been to London? ... How is it different from our village? What did you see when you mixed the salt into the water? ... What do you think happened?

Questions can be too easy, too difficult, too vague, asked too early in the teaching, or simply too many, with a deluge of questions used to produce the appearance of lively interactive teaching. Teachers need to consider their use of questions, and the questions they ask, thoughtfully. Effective questioning leads to good thinking. The revised version of Bloom's taxonomy (Anderson and Krathwohl, 2001) is helpful in evaluating questions in terms of the type of thinking they encourage:

Simple	1. remember	Recall information
	2. understand	Infer, compare, explain, classify, summarise
	3. apply	Use learned knowledge and understanding in new situations
	4. analyse	Examine how components of the learning relate to each other, and organise them
	5. evaluate	Make judgements, compare, draw conclusions
Complex	6. create	Reorganise elements in a new way, to produce something different

It is useful to remember that initiations – invitations to pupils to respond – do not have to be couched in a question format. Prompts such as 'Say a bit more about that', 'Go on' can give children an opportunity to develop their thinking, while non-verbal invitations such as a raised eyebrow, tilt of the head or nod can manage turn-taking effectively. It is also important to remember that if a question is worth asking it is worth giving children time to produce good responses. Most of the time children are expected to respond almost instantaneously, and they are not given time to process the question, think about it and produce a considered response. 'Wait time' is important here, but we tend to be uncomfortable with silence. It can be helpful to explain that this is what will happen: 'I'm going to ask you a question, and once you've heard it you'll have two minutes to think about it before I ask someone to answer.' Another option is the paired talk strategy, where children turn to their talk partner and discuss the question together before the teacher calls for responses. This can have a range of benefits: children have time to share and compare ideas; a child who could not have produced an answer alone is able to draw on the partner's thinking; children have far more opportunity to talk than if only whole-class discussion is used. However, it is important to monitor what is happening: are all pairs engaged in purposeful talk? If not, why not? How should the pairs be organised and should they be changed from time to time? What questions are worth some paired talk time and which are not: how long does it take, after all, to decide what sound you can hear in the middle of the word 'fish'? Too much recourse to talk partners can make a lesson very fragmented, so the strategy should be used thoughtfully.

Feedback

The third part of the three-part IRF exchange, following the initiation and response, is feedback, in which the teacher makes a comment on the pupil's response. This is often a simple repeating of what has been said, or non-specific positive feedback – praise – or, less often, feedback, which really helps to move the learning forward. Recent thinking (Hattie and Timperley, 2007) indicates that good feedback is one of the most effective ways of helping children learn, but current practice is often at odds with the research evidence.

Teachers should ask first whether they need to give evaluative feedback at all. A minimal response – 'Thank you', 'Anyone else?' 'Go on' is likely to open up the discussion rather than closing it down, and over time should make children less concerned about teacher judgements of their contributions, and therefore more adventurous in their thinking. Self-esteem should come from knowing others will listen carefully and critically to what you say, rather than being told you are brilliant every time you open your mouth. Wrong answers are another sensitive area in the classroom. The alarm and embarrassment that ensue suggest a social gaffe on a par with burping rather than simply thinking that 7 x 8 is 54. It is much more effective to say something like, 'No – have another think about it' than to pass the question hastily to another pupil. Getting it wrong should be an every-day part of classroom life – and indeed an important part of learning.

Focused feedback may reflect back to the pupil what they have done but will be of most value if it can develop thinking and learning through a new initiation. For example:

'You've given three reasons why you were surprised by the ending of the story' is an example of useful feedback, but

'Which of your three reasons do you think is the most powerful?' adds a challenge.

Children's questions

It was said earlier that at home children ask far more questions than they do at school. These are not all of the 'Can I have a drink/Where's my foot-ball kit/Are we nearly there? type. Children ask huge numbers of questions each day, and they range from the profound to the bizarre to the awkward. In school, however, opportunities for asking questions seem very limited, and children soon begin to feel that their role is to answer, not ask, questions. On the occasions when children are required to ask questions, adults are sometimes disappointed by their quality – though any teacher trying to plan some inference questions for a guided reading session might sympa-thise. Thinking of thought-provoking, probing questions is not easy.

It is important for children to have opportunities to generate questions – but the beginning of a topic, which is so often when this is done, may not be the best time. It is hard to have worthwhile questions about a topic we know nothing about, and children may need to research a little before they really can see what questions need to be asked.

Managing talk in the classroom

With often around 30 potential participants in classroom talk, managing the talk is clearly a necessity. This involves managing turn-taking in whole-class discussion and also strategies for ensuring children get many opportunities to talk. Typically, children have indicated their readiness to participate by putting a hand up, but this is a system with many difficulties. First, some children are reluctant to nominate themselves in this way, and effectively they withdraw from classroom talk. The danger here is twofold: that because they do not expect to participate they do not engage as fully with what is going on, and also that teachers have no idea of their level of under-standing. Assessment may be extremely unreliable if it is based on the answers of the arm-waving minority. Second, when children have volun-teered to respond they are laying claim to having a good answer, and it can then be hard to find that you are wrong. Third, there may be resentment of the quick-thinking children with good memories who are able to dominate classroom discourse when it is managed by 'hands-up'. Finally, some children really want to participate, but don't have the answer or cannot formulate one quickly enough. These are the ones who may put their hands up, but when chosen subside with an embarrassed 'I've forgotten'.

Teacher strategies for avoiding the problems of hands-up include deliberately asking children who do not raise their hands. This can cause its own problems, from a series of mumbled 'don't knows' to the gambler who concludes that if he waves energetically enough he will never be selected, and will be safe. Increasingly, therefore, hands-up is only used as it might be in an adult context, to get a quick response to a real question – 'Who's ready to move on to the next bit?' or 'Who's read anything by Philip Pullman?' – or as a mechanism for pupils to indicate that they have a comment or wish to contribute to a discussion. Instead, a no-hands-up policy sets up the expectation that any pupil may be called on to respond; opting out is not an option. Some teachers use a set of lolly sticks with the children's names on to select respondents randomly; others colour-code the lolly sticks so the selection is rather less random than it appears to the children.

Developing group talk

It is an interesting feature of primary classrooms that they are often arranged as if group talk and group activity are the most common approaches used; children sit at tables of four or six, facing each other, sometimes even with their backs to the 'front' of the classroom, where the interactive whiteboard is placed and where the teacher usually stands. Yet such group work is often quite rare. Even when group tasks are set, one can sometimes see tables where the children are not functioning as a group at all, groups which are dominated by one individual, and groups which are arguing about what to do or how to do it. Dawes et al. (2004) suggest that group size is important, and that three is an ideal number, yet groups are often double this size; also that it is preferable that the children are not friends, as this can result in uncritical agreement. However, this is probably a question of personality rather than relationships; some friends enjoy heated debates while some relative strangers would find it very difficult to disagree with a point of view they do not share. Of course, group membership needs to be considered, and if the class usually works in what are commonly referred to as ability groups, there is no reason why these groupings should be used for group talk. In addition, good group talk does not just happen; children need to be trained to do it. The Primary National Strategy *Speaking, Listening, Learning* materials (DfES, 2003) included useful guidance on developing children's skills in this area, although the suggested differentiation of roles within the group – leader, scribe, observer and so on – perhaps actually limited the opportunity for real group talk. Probably the best strategy is to have children produce their own ground rules for group talk, though these could usefully include rules such as:

- everyone has to join in and everyone must be listened to;
- all ideas must be considered and all ideas can be questioned;
- all points of view must be supported with reasons;
- the group must agree its decisions.

Ground rules could arise from a discussion or by children selecting a limited number of rules from a longer list, as suggested by Dawes et al. (2004).

The focus of group talk is likely to be a group discussion or an investigation – in other words, an activity where children can support and challenge each other's thinking. This is what Barnes (2008) describes as exploratory talk, also referred to as process talk, which has already been discussed in Chapter 3 on talk for learning, but Barnes contrasts this talk with presentational talk, an example of which might be a group member reporting back to the whole class, and this will be discussed later.

Case study   Small group discussions

Mary Jane Drummond (1993) gives a fascinating account of small group discussions in the Sheffield infant school where she was head-teacher in her classic book *Assessing Children's Learning*. For four years she regularly brought together groups of children aged from four to seven, for up to three-quarters of an hour at a time. She began by explaining what discussion was, and what the children's role was – to think of ideas, to share them, and to question and comment on the ideas of other group members. Topics were negotiated between group members and Drummond herself, and Drummond's role was simply to record contributions to the discussion on large sheets of paper, so that the ideas were preserved. Topics were varied and surprising: saying goodbye; stripes; things tortoises can't do; umbrellas; white; silence. The account of the discussions is a moving and inspiring example of how children can share their thoughts and develop their thinking in a host of ways – comparing, challenging, categorising, generalising, qualifying, analysing, justifying and more.

Recording children's oral contributions is a powerful way of showing that we value what they say, not just what they put on paper. This could be audio-recording or video-recording as well as making a written record. All of them allow children to return to their talk as a starting point for further talk, or to evaluate it.

Group talk strategies

There are many useful techniques that can be used to develop group discussion, which Jolliffe (2007) explores in some depth. These include:

- think-pair-share, where children work on a task individually, then discuss it with a partner, then the pairs form groups of four to discuss the views of the two pairs;
- snowballing, where children work first in pairs, then pairs join into fours, fours into eights and so on;
- jigsawing, where children work in groups, each with a different aspect of the topic to work on, and then new groups are formed, each containing one member from each of the original expert groups. Ideas are shared, then the original groups may re-form to report back from the mixed groups; rainbowing follows a similar formula;
- envoying, where after the group discussion representatives move around the other groups to share ideas.

Approaches to talk in the classroom: philosophy for children, dialogic teaching and sustained shared thinking

Three approaches to classroom talk which have been very influential are philosophy for children, dialogic teaching and sustained shared thinking.

Philosophy for children

Philosophy for children is an approach developed by Matthew Lipman, who taught philosophy at Columbia University. Lipman believed that philosophy can teach children to think, and that the 'community of enquiry' in which children discuss philosophical concepts is central to this. The approach was brought to Scotland in 1990 by Dr Catherine McCall, who worked with Lipman, and there has been considerable interest in philosophy for children since then. Even young children were shown to be capable of abstract thought, and indeed to enjoy discussion of difficult concepts. The approach develops higher order thinking skills and also leads to improved oracy skills and improved academic attainment.

Dialogic teaching

Dialogic teaching (see also Chapter 3) is an approach which began with Robin Alexander's (2001) major cross-cultural study of primary teaching in five countries and cultures, including Russia, the United States and England. Alexander noted that in whole-class teaching in Russian classrooms there were longer sequences of talk with one child, with a clear focus on developing understanding. Children came to the front of the room to speak, and were expected to speak clearly and audibly from a young age. Not all children spoke in every lesson; they were seen as representatives of the whole class rather than individuals. The characteristics of dialogic teaching are that it is:

- collective – children are learning together rather than as individuals;
- reciprocal – teacher and pupils listen to each other's ideas;
- supportive – children do not worry about getting the right answer;
- cumulative – learners build on each other's ideas to develop lines of thinking;
- purposeful – talk has a clear educational aim.

Projects in North Yorkshire and Barking and Dagenham provided professional development for teachers and opportunities to study and monitor their own practice and its impact on learning (Alexander, 2008) and there were many positive findings, but some teachers found dialogic teaching more challenging than others, and Alexander felt that teacher feedback still did not move learning forward often enough.

Sustained shared thinking

There is a parallel between dialogic teaching and the Early Years concept of sustained shared thinking which came out of the Effective Provision of Pre-School Education (EPPE) research project (Sylva et al., 2004). Researchers analysed talk between practitioners and young children, and looked for sequences of talk where the adult helped children to develop their understanding through responses which built on what the children said rather than simply echoing it, or which challenged them. The research evidence showed that even in the best settings such talk was rare.

Presentational talk

The 2014 Primary National Curriculum states that children should be 'taught to speak clearly and convey ideas confidently using Standard English' (DfE, 2013: 10). The programme of study for English refers to children taking part in presentations and debates, and speaking audibly and fluently. This suggests talk in more formal contexts, where there has often been opportunity for some level of preparation. Presentational talk is important and careful planning is needed to ensure children have the time and opportunity to practise and develop their skills. This can be difficult if everything is done in the whole-class context; there simply is not enough time for every child to speak at any length to the whole class regularly enough to develop confidence and skills. Circle time can be problematic in this respect; because every pupil has to be given a turn, turns are of necessity short and often very repetitive.

The spectacle of every child trying to think of something nice to say about the child who happens to be sitting next to them can be both tedious and painful. However, it can be used to ensure that at the least each child speaks audibly to the group as a whole. Observation of a Year 1 circle time showed that while some children were still very shy, others introduced themselves and their neighbours to the group with some aplomb: 'My name is Martin, and this is Kennedy and this is Billy!', one child announced, accompanying the words with sweeping gestures. But too often the children who are articulate and fluent have developed their skills outside school while those who do not have the same opportunities at home remain reluctant and inarticulate speakers in formal settings. When it comes to choosing children to take the starring roles in class assemblies, plays and so on the ones who most need the practice are least likely to be chosen. It is sensible therefore to use group work for presentational talk as well as process talk, to give children that practice. The pupil who reports group views to another group has had time to consider what to say, and needs to be clear, concise and convincing.

Final thoughts...

A final note: it is useful and interesting for children to reflect on language use. They might consider and discuss such questions as:

- Why is talk useful, and what would we do if we couldn't talk?
- How do babies and young children communicate? How do we learn to talk?
- Do people talk differently in different situations?
- Do people talk differently in different places?
- Do people of different ages talk differently?
- What are the differences between talk and writing?

It is also useful to collect and define words about talk – opinion, argument, assert, challenge, negotiate, consider – so that children have the vocabulary to discuss their own language. For both pupils and teachers, awareness of how we use language can be the first step to becoming a more skilful language user.

References

Alexander, R. (2001) *Culture and Pedagogy: international comparisons in primary education*. Oxford: Blackwell.

Alexander, R. (2008) Culture, dialogue and learning: notes on an emerging pedagogy, in Mercer, N. and Hodkinson, S. (eds) *Exploring Talk in School*. London: Sage.

Anderson, L.W. and Krathwohl, D.R. et al. (2001) *A Taxonomy for Learning, Teaching and Assessing: a revision of Bloom's taxonomy of educational objectives*. New York: Longman.

Barnes, D. (2008) Exploratory talk for learning, in Mercer, N. and Hodkinson, S. (eds) *Exploring Talk in School*. London: Sage.

Brien, J. (2012) *Teaching Primary English*. London: Sage.

Dawes, L., Mercer, N. and Wegerif, R. (2004) *Thinking Together: a programme of activities for developing thinking skills at KS2*. Birmingham: The Questions Publishing Company.

DfES (2003) *Speaking, Listening, Learning: working with children in Key Stage 1 and 2*. Norwich: Department for Education and Skills.

DFE (2013) *The 2014 Primary National Curriculum in England Key Stages 1 & 2 Framework*. Romsey: Shurville Publishing.

Drummond, M.J. (1993) *Assessing Children's Learning*. London: David Fulton.

Flanders, N.A. (1970) *Analyzing Teaching Behaviour*. Reading, MA: Addison-Wesley.

Hanks, P. (1989) *The Collins School Dictionary*. Glasgow: Collins.

Hattie, J. and Timperley, H. (2007) The power of feedback. *Review of Educational Research*, 77 (1): 81–112.

Jolliffe, W. (2007) *Cooperative Learning in the Classroom: putting it into practice*. London: Paul Chapman.

Knight, L. and Delahunty, A. (1997) *The Junior School Dictionary*. Jordan Hill: Ginn.

Mroz, M., Smith, F. and Hardman, F. The discourse of the Literacy Hour. *Cambridge Journal of Education*, 30: 379–90.

Sinclair, J. and Coulthard, M. (1992) Towards an analysis of discourse, in M. Coulthard (ed.) *Advances in Spoken Discourse Analysis*. London: Routledge.

Smith, F., Hardman, F., Wall, K. and Mroz, M. (2004) Interactive whole class teaching in the National Numeracy and Literacy Strategies. *British Educational Research Journal*, 30(3): 395–411.

Sylva, K., Melhuish, E., Sammons, P., Siraj-Blatchford, I. and Taggart, B. (2004) *The Effective Provision of Pre-School Education*. Nottingham: DfES Publications.

Wragg, E.C. and Brown, G. (1993) *Questioning*. London: Routledge.

Wragg, E.C. and Brown, G. (2001a) *Explaining in the Primary School*. London: Routledge/Falmer.

Wragg, E.C. and Brown, G. (2001b) *Questioning in the Primary School*. London: Routledge/Falmer.

CHAPTER 5

LANGUAGE AND COMMUNICATION IN THE ENGLISH CURRICULUM

Despite an apparent reduction in the emphasis on speaking and listening in the English National Curriculum (DfE, 2013), oracy remains at the heart of children's learning.

If we simply look at the number of times different aspects of English are mentioned, the impression is that speaking and listening are accorded little status:

Writing	140
Reading	115
Spelling	101
Books	60
Grammar	50
Punctuation	33

Listening	19
Poems	14
Poetry	11
Drama	8
Speaking	6
Literacy	2
Literature	2

(Waugh et al., 2014: 2)

In this chapter, however, we will show that oracy underpins all aspects of English, helping to develop children's ability to write well, their reading comprehension skills, and their understanding of spelling, punctuation and grammar.

Talk for Writing

Writing often can, and probably should, be a solitary and silent activity. Many writers like to find a quiet and perhaps special place where they can concentrate without distractions. Roald Dahl, for example, had a summer house in his garden where he created many of the best known characters in children's literature. In English primary schools, Year 6 children are required to write under examination conditions without support and discussion. However, before we can write independently, certain skills need to be acquired. The *Talk for Writing* project identified the following as qualities of good writers, and stated that they:

- enjoy writing and find the process creative, enriching and fulfilling;
- read widely, recognise good writing, and understand what makes it good;
- are aware of the key features of different genres and text types;
- learn about the skills of writing from their reading and draw (consciously or unconsciously) upon its models in their own work;
- have 'something to say' (a purpose and audience);
- know how to develop their ideas;
- know how to plan and prepare for writing;
- make informed choices about what they are writing, as they write (for example, about vocabulary, grammar, text structure, etc.);
- understand how to reflect upon, refine and improve their own work;
- can respond to the constructive criticism of others. (DCSF, 2008: 3)

The *Talk for Writing* authors argued that many of the above processes are internal and automatic for experienced writers who can, for example, hold an internal dialogue with themselves to make choices about vocabulary, phrasing and sentence construction. For developing writers, however, these processes need to be demonstrated within a supportive learning context. Through shared writing, experienced writers can model the thought processes they engage in when constructing a piece of writing. They can ask themselves questions (aloud for the children's benefit) and can show that they reflect upon what they have written and make changes in order to improve it.

Talk for Writing involves developing, through talk, the thinking and creative processes involved in being a writer. It is embedded within each phase of a teaching sequence for writing, which takes children from experiencing text to observing writing to writing with support to independent writing. Guidance for *Talk for Writing* states that talk needs to occur:

- **during reading**: when familiarising with the genre/text type and its key features; when responding to, exploring and drawing on models;
- **before writing**: when generating ideas, preparing for and planning writing;
- **during all stages of writing** (teacher's demonstration and scribing, and children's supported, guided and independent writing): when making the choices involved in creating, developing and improving texts;
- **after writing**: when reflecting on and learning from a writing experience.

There are three levels of talk:

- **Teacher talk**: The verbalisation of the reader's or writer's thought processes as the teacher is demonstrating, modelling and discussing.
- **Supported pupil talk**: Structured and scaffolded opportunities for children to develop and practise *Talk for Writing* through class and group conversations and activities.
- **Independent pupil talk**: Opportunities for children to develop and practise *Talk for Writing* in pairs and small groups, independent of the teacher. (DCSF, 2008: 5)

In order to illustrate how talk can be an integral part of the writing sequence, a process is described in the case study below.

Case study   *Jessica's Other World*

Laura, an NQT, used the extract below as a starting point for a project on other world stories with her Year 5 class. She planned to explore other books, including *Tom's Midnight Garden*, *Alice's Adventures in Wonderland* and the *Narnia* series, and wished to use an example of such a text as a starting point. Laura planned to read the story opening to promote discussion about both content and presentation and then lead into shared writing in which she would model a writer's thought processes, followed by guided and independent work.

CHAPTER I
JESSICA'S OTHER HOUSE

It was on a dark and foggy March night, when Jessica was lying awake listening to Ellie's snoring, that her adventure began. Her legs hung over the edge of the bed, because her two sisters had taken up most of the room, and she was cold and uncomfortable. The bed was old-fashioned and had long legs which raised it nearly a metre off the floor. Jessica decided that she would wrap herself in the spare blanket and try to sleep under the bed – at least there would be more room! The springs creaked as she crept out of bed, but her sisters hardly stirred. As quietly as she could, Jessica slid under the bed and rolled herself up in a rather musty smelling blanket.

The floor was hard and bare and the floorboards smelled of ancient varnish. She closed her eyes and tried counting sheep. She had just managed to visualise dozens of the woolly creatures, leaping one by one through a gap in a hawthorn hedge, when she sensed something sticking into her back. She felt around on the floor and found what seemed like a large ring. Rolling over, Jessica tried to pick up the ring but it was attached to the floor. She noticed, though, that the floor seemed to lift a little as she tugged.

Jessica was now wide awake and curious. Next to the bed, on Grace's side, was a small torch which the girls used for reading under the blankets when their mother told them to put the light out. Jessica crawled under the bed until she came out next to Grace, and she reached for the torch. It was too dark to see anything and, just as she put her hand out to pick the torch up from the bedside table, she lost her grip and the torch clattered to the floor. She froze. Her sisters stirred and Ellie coughed, but after what seemed like an hour, although it was probably only a few minutes, the girls settled back to their rhythmic breathing and snoring.

Jessica reached her hand along the floor until she felt the torch and she carefully picked it up. Under the bed, she shone the torch

(Continued)

(Continued)

around until it lighted the area where she had been lying. There was a ring. It was about six centimetres in diameter, made of a dark metal, and part of it was fixed to the floor with a metal band. Jessica looked more closely and saw that there was a narrow gap in the floor boards around the ring and that this formed a square about half a metre across. She had never looked under the bed so closely before and she suspected that no-one else had either. When the girls tidied their room, they usually threw the items which caused the mess under the bed and forgot about them. She could certainly never remember the bed being moved.

Jessica took the ring in her hands and pulled. The floor boards creaked slightly and a square of floor lifted. She only raised it a little, but as she did so she noticed a bright light shining from three sides of the square. It was difficult to find enough room under the bed to pull at the ring properly and she had to lie on her side. Even then, she kept bumping her head on the springs and she was afraid that she would wake her sisters. Finally, she managed to lift the boards enough to slide a slipper into the gap to prop them up. Once she had done this, it was possible to slide the wood away from its position. She took the ring in both hands and rolled away onto her back. As she did so, the wooden square moved and the underside of the bed was suddenly illuminated.

Jessica rolled back and saw that a square of light had been revealed. She turned onto her stomach and peered into it.

(Taken from Waugh, D. (2016) *Jessica's Other World.* Bishop's Castle: Constance Books.)

During and just after reading the story opening to the class, Laura discussed vocabulary and phrasing, as well as events. She drew attention to words, including: *snoring, old-fashioned, ancient, varnish, tugged, clattered, rhythmic, curious* and *suspected*. They talked about how Jessica might feel as the events unfolded, and she encouraged them to predict what might happen next. Finally, she asked a child to take on the role of Jessica and be in the 'hot-seat' to answer questions in role.

This was followed by structured opportunities for small group discussions in which children speculated and made notes on what might happen next.

Laura then modelled writing by creating her own two sentences to continue the story, before asking children to suggest what she might write next. As she did this, she spoke her thoughts aloud so that children could see how she weighed up options for vocabulary, phrasing, punctuation and spelling. Children were then offered the choice of continuing the story and writing the next section based upon what Laura had written, or they could continue from the end of the extract. Before they began to write, Laura asked children to discuss and try out their ideas on each other and to make notes of any good ideas suggested by others.

Some children worked in pairs to write, while a small group worked with Laura as a guided group and another worked with the teaching assistant. Throughout the writing, there were frequent pauses for people to share their ideas and for Laura to read out some examples. Finally, the class came together to discuss what they had done and to share ideas and talk about what helped them to write well and what inhibited them. There was general agreement that having someone to discuss ideas with and get feedback from was useful and enabled them to produce better writing.

Laura's approach to teaching writing made the process easier for some children who would have been challenged by having to write alone, but it also enabled children to share ideas and discuss presentation, including grammar, spelling and punctuation. She also gave the children a purpose and audience for their writing by making it clear that they would be sharing their ideas both during the writing and in a plenary. Martin et al. (2012) stress the importance of purpose in motivating people to write both for external sources (a letter to someone) and internal (a personal journal, notes to remind us about things, etc.). They conclude: *If we add together purpose and audience (why am I writing and who will be reading it) we find ourselves considering the best ways to construct the text we want to write* (Martin et al., 2012: 36).

In the next section, we consider how children's literature can act as a stimulus for discussion, while developing their comprehension skills and broadening their reading experiences.

Story reading and language development

Many student teachers complain that they cannot meet their courses' requirements that they read regularly to children because class teachers say there isn't sufficient time in a crowded curriculum for this 'luxury'. This is unfortunate, since listening to stories produces significant benefits for children as it enables them to:

- hear a story being read well;
- enjoy stories and gain an appetite for independent reading;
- gain access to stories and language usage which they might not be able to read independently;
- experience new vocabulary and phrasing;
- develop listening skills;
- develop comprehension skills through discussion of texts with the teacher and each other;
- develop ideas for their own writing;
- engage in follow-up activities including drama and role play.

One of the aspects of the 2013 English National Curriculum which pleased many educators was the emphasis placed on reading aloud to children. This continues into Year 6 where we find:

> Even though pupils can now read independently, reading aloud to them should include whole books so that they meet books and authors that they might not choose to read themselves. (DfE, 2013: 43)

Too often, however, children's experience of hearing a story is through excerpts read to them as part of shared reading. The opportunities above are rich and fundamental to children's language development. Look at the story opening below and consider the opportunities for language development which could emanate from reading it to children:

CHAPTER ONE
It's not a proper game if she plays

"It's not a proper game if she plays!" Adam Stevens stood with his foot on the ball and his hands on his hips.

"Go on, let her," said Ryan Jones.

Lauren Morris looked longingly towards the football pitch, where about twenty boys had stopped their game when she had asked to play.

"Even if she wasn't a girl, she's too small and she'd get hurt," said Faisal Ahmed, who was eleven.

"She's bigger than me," piped up Sam Bell.

"Everyone's bigger than you, Belly!" chorused about five people together.

Lauren longed to play football. She had taken months to pluck up the courage to ask the boys if she could join in with their daily game after school, and now she seemed likely to be rejected. She was sure she would be good at soccer. She had watched endless videos of matches, and she spent hours practising her ball skills in her tiny back yard and in the passageway behind her house, and on the wasteland next to an old, disused factory near her house.

She had often watched the boys from a distance and she was certain that she was more skilful than most of them. The trouble was, she had never played in a game. She could dribble in and out of the obstacle courses she set up for herself using plastic bottles and drinks cans, and she could trap and volley the ball as she bounced it off the brick wall of the old factory. What she did not know was if she could use her skills when other people were trying to take the ball from her.

The boys began to get restless. They wanted to get on with their game and Lauren's request had stopped them.

"Why shouldn't she play?" asked Mark Langley. "Just because she's a girl, it doesn't mean she's no good."

"Just because you fancy her," sneered Michael Benson, who had no time to say any more before Mark pushed him and they began rolling around on the floor fighting. The others quickly pulled them apart before they had chance to hurt each other much.

"This is typical of what happens when you let girls play boys' games," said Adam Stevens. "I say we get on with the game and tell her to get lost."

(Taken from Waugh, D. (2015) *"Girls Can't Play Football!"*. Bishop's Castle: Constance Books.)

Brown (1997) used the following questions as a starting point for discussions:

- Has anything that happened in the book ever happened to you?
- Were there any patterns or connections that you noticed?
- Was there anything that puzzled you?
- When you first saw the book, what kind of book did you expect it to be?

Consider the last question first. The title of the book is provocative, yet it is set within quotation marks and has an exclamation mark: what might children discuss?

Can they relate to the characters, even at this early stage in the story? Could you introduce hot-seating (see below) and get children to answer questions in role, or even ask questions in role? Can they picture the scene? Is there any vocabulary or phrasing which they are unsure about? Are there any similarities to any other stories they know?

By getting children to explore the text in this way at the outset, we set them up to be able to read and understand the story as it progresses. They also develop the ability to infer meaning from the text. Krispal (2008) described the outcomes of inference training conducted by McGee and Johnson in 2003, which replicated Yuill and Oakhill's 1988 work. They found that inference training *raised performance in less skilled comprehenders by 20 months, while comprehension practice had resulted in an improvement of 10 months* (Krispal, 2008: 24). The inference training involved the following steps:

> **lexical training**: explaining the function and added meaning of individual words. For example, in the following: 'Sleepy Tom was late for school again', attention was drawn to the additional information that can be gleaned from 'again' (habitually), 'sleepy' (up late the night before), 'Tom' (boy).
>
> **question generation**: after instruction on the meaning of the question words 'who', 'when', 'why' etc, pupils were given examples of how questions can be derived from a text. Then pupils generated their own questions from a text and others answered.
>
> **prediction**: sentences were obscured from a text and pupils guessed the missing segments by inference and deduction from the surrounding text. (Krispal, 2008: 25)

So sharing stories with children has the potential to enhance their communication skills and their comprehension ability. It also develops children's ability to construct and remember stories, which is fundamental to conversation. Consider the conversations you have had with friends recently. How often does this include relating a tale of something that happened to one of you, perhaps followed by the other telling a similar or related tale in return?

Telling tales

Pie Corbett emphasises the importance of being able to tell stories and understanding how stories work. Children, he argues, need to build up a bank of stories they know and can repeat and adapt. In the case study below, a teacher develops children's story-telling in a simple yet engaging and imaginative way.

Case study   Telling people's stories in first person

Eve wanted her Year 4 class to think about the characteristics of a good story and to engage with telling a story for an audience. She knew that many children would be reluctant to tell stories to the whole class, so she used a strategy she had learnt on her PGCE course which involved people telling a neighbour a short story of something which had happened to them. She modelled this by telling the class about a walk she had been on when she had seen a snake. She varied her tone of voice to show when she was nervous and when she was relieved to discover the snake was a harmless grass snake, which quickly vanished into the long grass when it realised she was near.

Eve explained that stories didn't have to be very long and could be about very ordinary, everyday events, but that they should try to make them interesting for the listener. She asked the children to sit in a circle in pairs, with one person being A and the other B, and to take turns to tell a short story about something they had done. They were allowed no more than two minutes each. Once everyone had told a story, Eve asked all the As to stand up and move two places to the left so that they had a new partner. The children then had to tell the stories they had heard from their first partner in the first person, as if the events had happened to them. Some found this difficult at first and kept going into the third person, but by the time the As had moved on three times and told and retold the stories, everyone was able to tell the stories properly.

At the end of the session, Eve asked people to tell a story in the first person to the whole class and insisted that the person whose story it was did not interrupt to correct the tale. The resulting stories brought laughter and lots of discussion about ways of remembering key facts and keeping to the first person.

Activities such as Eve's help inculcate in children an appreciation of the components of story-telling and develop awareness of ways in which they can make their stories more engaging and hold the attention of listeners. By allowing children to relate stories to each other in pairs, before or instead of to the whole class, we can develop their confidence and enable them to be more assured of an attentive audience. The oral rehearsal of stories prior to writing can be invaluable preparation for successful writing. By articulating their ideas orally in a sequential way, writers are effectively planning and will therefore be less likely to reach points where they simply cannot think what to write next.

This oral rehearsal can be extended through the use of drama, which has the potential to develop both children's oral and written communication skills.

Drama and written communication

Clipson-Boyles (2012: 83) suggests children can 'write before the drama', 'write during the drama' and 'write after the drama'. They might write a note or message that sets up a drama; they can write as the drama is developing, perhaps as one of the characters; and can write reflectively after the drama.

Of course, not all drama work will involve or lead to written work, but drama can be a powerful tool for developing story-telling and an appreciation of audience and so can have strong links to writing when appropriate.

Engaging in dramatic activities can also help children to remember stories, whether these are based on works of fiction or historical events. As Johnson (2006: 100) argues: 'If teachers are to create "sparks that make learning vivid" in the classroom, then drama is the box of matches'.

The figures at the beginning of this chapter may suggest that drama is a low priority in the 2013 English National Curriculum, but the authors do recognise its value. In Year 2, for example, it states:

> Role-play and other drama techniques can help pupils to identify with and explore characters. In these ways, they extend their understanding of what they read and have opportunities to try out the language they have listened to. (DfE, 2013: 28)

Barrs (2001) worked with Year 5 children exploring the difference between oral and written story-telling. A key finding from the project was that when children worked on the themes of a text in a drama workshop they found it easier to understand the text later. Barrs (2001: 56) maintained: *This had a big impact on the children, who seemed to relate much more closely and personally to this text because they had already 'lived through' some of the events and situations.* Interestingly, the authors of the 2013 English National Curriculum also recognise the value of drama in developing writing:

> Drama and role-play can contribute to the quality of pupils' writing by providing opportunities for pupils to develop and order their ideas by playing roles and improvising scenes in various settings. (DfE, 2013: 30)

In Years 3 and 4, the National Curriculum states that 'pupils should become more familiar with and confident in using language in a greater variety of situations, for a variety of audiences and purposes, including through drama, formal presentations and debate' (DfE, 2013: 34).

By engaging in drama activities, children can internalise processes and sequences as well as stories, enabling them to be able to record these in writing later where appropriate. For example, they could enact the life cycle of a butterfly using pictorial representations and body shapes, with a narrator explaining the process to the audience.

Learning through talk

Finally, it is worth exploring the value of talk in investigations in English. These might include children exploring texts to find different ways of opening stories, or examples of variations in word order, such as fronting adverbials.

They might also discuss and investigate authors' use of descriptive language or of connecting words and phrases. In the case study below, children work co-operatively to explore spelling patterns and to draw conclusions about an aspect of English spelling.

Case study   Spelling investigation: which letters don't appear at the end of English words?

Amira's Year 1 class had been learning systematic phonics using the school's scheme, which was largely based on *Letters and Sounds* (DfES, 2007). Most children were growing in confidence in letter sound correspondences and their writing was increasingly readable and confidently produced, despite spelling errors which resulted from a literal approach to spelling. For example, in many pieces of writing typical errors included: *ov* for *of*, *hej* for *hedge*, *hav* for *have*, and *luv* for *love*.

Amira did not wish to discourage children from writing and was happy to accept some spelling errors as part of emergent writing. However, she felt she could help children to develop greater appreciation of possible spellings for some phonemes if she involved groups in a spelling investigation. She therefore asked children to look at books, signs, lists and other sources and challenged them to find three letters which never appear at the ends of English words. Before they began, Amira asked the groups to speculate on what the letters might be and then test their hypotheses as they looked at texts. She found it interesting to hear their ideas and the way other group members responded with examples to disprove them. For example, children suggested *x* did not appear at the ends of words, but were reminded about *box, fox* and *fix; z* but *buzz* and *fizz* were cited; and *i* but were given the example of *taxi*.

The investigation promoted a lot of discussion and children happily skimmed through texts and pointed out words, some of which they could not actually read properly, to disprove each other's theories. Finally, she brought the groups together to share their findings. None had found a word ending with *j* or *v*, and only one had found a word ending with *q*: *Iraq*, which Amira pointed out was not an English word but the name of a country. There was some discussion about words like *satnav* but Amira explained that these were abbreviations of longer words.

Having established that English words did not end with *j, v* or *q*, Amira then asked children to attempt to spell some of the words which had been misspelled using these letters at the end. There was discussion about alternatives and Amira was able to show children correct spellings.

The example above shows the value of children thinking about spelling and then working together to discuss and test their ideas. Pierce and Gilles (2008: 45) maintain that: *When students go public with their work, they will begin to see that work from a new perspective.*

By investigating and drawing conclusions, they are more likely to internalise what they have learned than if they were simply told the answer. Furthermore, the teacher is able to identify children's misconceptions and then address them and adjust planning to meet specific needs. Following the success of the investigations, Amira set up similar activities using digraphs. In one, she asked a group to look at double letters and use simple dictionaries to find which double letters do not appear at the beginnings of words (e.g. *bb, cc, dd, ff, gg, hh*) and which did (e.g. *aardvark, eerie, llama, ooze*), and which did not appear at the end of words. They also looked at consonant digraphs such as *sh, ch, ck*, to see which could begin and end words and which could not. This kind of activity might be used by different age groups. As Browne (2009: 136) maintains:

> Developing children's awareness of words and letters benefits all children regardless of the spelling stage that they have reached. Simple, everyday activities which encourage children to examine and talk about words can be used with even the youngest children.

An example could be inviting a Year 4 class to devise a rule for making words which end with 'y' plural. If a selection of words is provided for groups of children (e.g. boy, day, key, baby, lady, monkey, donkey, toy, etc.), they can be challenged to find the plurals of each word and then determine why for some the 'y' is removed and '-ies' added, while for others the plural is made simply by adding an 's'. Once such spelling generalisations have been discovered and discussed with the teacher, children are much more likely to remember them than if they were simply told them.

Final thoughts...

In this chapter, we have explored the value of talk for learning by focusing on the English curriculum. By encouraging children to work collaboratively and co-operatively, we not only enable them to share ideas and learn together, but also help develop their language and communication skills and enable them to internalise new learning.

References

Barrs, M (2001) The reader in the writer. *Reading Literacy and Language*. 34(2), 54-60. London: CLPE.

Brown, A. (1997) Transforming schools into communities of thinking and learning about serious matters. *American Psychologist,* 52: 399–413.

Browne, A. (2009) *Developing Language and Literacy 3–8*. London: Sage.

Clipson-Boyles, S. (2012) *Teaching Primary English Through Drama*. London: David Fulton.

Corbett, P. *Talk 4 Writing on Today's Schools*. Available at: www.youtube.com/watch?v=Ej-UHjxmHC8 (accessed 17.9.2015).

DCSF (2008) *Talk for Writing*. Nottingham: DCSF.

DfE (2013) *The National Curriculum in England Key Stages 1 and 2 Framework Document*. London: DfE.

DfES (2007) *Letters and Sounds: principles and practice of high quality phonics*. London: DfES.

Johnson, C. (2006) in D. Jones and P. Hodson (eds) *Unlocking Speaking and Listening*. London: David Fulton.

Krispal, A. (2008) *Effective Teaching of Inference Skills for Reading Literature Review*. National Foundation for Educational Research. London: DCSF.

McGee, A. and Johnson, H. (2003) The effect of inference training on skilled and less skilled comprehenders. *Educational Psychology*, 23 (1): 49–59.

Martin, T., Lovat, C. and Purnell, G. (2012) *The Really Useful Literacy Book*. London: Routledge.

Pierce, K. and Gilles, C. (2008) in N. Mercer and S. Hodgkinson (eds) *Exploring Talk in School*. London: Sage.

Waugh, D. (2015) *'Girls Can't Play Football!'* Bishop's Castle: Constance Books. Extract first published in DCSF (2009) *Developing Literacy in Initial Teacher Training DVD*. London: DCSF.

Waugh, D. (2016) *Jessica's Other World*. Bishop's Castle: Constance Books. Extract first published in Waugh, D. (2000) *Further Curriculum Bank Writing Activities Key Stage Two*. Leamington Spa: Scholastic.

Waugh, D., Jolliffe, W. and Allott, K. (eds) (2014*) Primary English for Trainee Teachers*. London: Sage.

CHAPTER 6

PLANNING FOR AND ASSESSING SPEAKING AND LISTENING

Brien (2012: 19) describes speaking and listening in the classroom as both omnipresent and neglected. She suggests that because there is so much talk in the classroom it is easy to assume that it is well catered for, whereas as we have discovered in previous chapters, this may not always be the case. Assessment of speaking and listening is much more difficult than assessment of, say, children's spelling or their understanding of number. Nor is it easy to plan effectively for progression in speaking and listening: although we would hope and expect to see changes over time, it is probably not realistic to claim that within a single lesson, or even a unit, one can see measurable learning. (This is, of course, true of many other areas of learning, and is one of the difficult issues for teachers, which has developed as a result of a strong focus in recent years on pupil progress.) It is also the case that with the demands that planning and assessment place on teachers, what is needed is a manageable approach. This chapter will argue that while teachers need good subject knowledge, a clear understanding of progression in speaking and listening and realistic expectations, planning and assessment need not be yet another significant burden.

The view of planning and assessment as a cycle suggests that there is no natural starting point – do we begin with planning, or do we suggest that no planning can be effective without meaningful assessment as a basis? The chapter will begin by examining National Curriculum expectations for speaking and listening, and considering what progression in speaking and listening from Foundation Stage to the end of Key Stage 2 might look like. With that picture of overall goals in mind, we will move on to consider how speaking and listening can be built into the curriculum rather than bolted on to it, and what assessment is necessary to support effective teaching and learning. Throughout, the emphasis will be on planning for and assessing speaking and listening, not planning and assessing learning through talk. This is an important distinction.

Chapter 1 has already outlined progression in the four strands of language development during the Foundation Stage. Language development after the first few years does not continue at the same pace, and changes are more subtle than the change, say, from one-word utterances to complex grammatical structures. It makes sense therefore to consider expectations at longer intervals as children grow older, and particularly at the end of each key stage.

The National Curriculum programme of study for English (DfE, 2013: 13) makes reference to children learning to speak fluently in order to *communicate their ideas and emotions*; to *use discussion in order to learn; they should be able to elaborate and explain clearly their understanding and ideas*; to *understand and use the conventions for discussion and debate* and to *participate in and gain knowledge, skills and understanding associated with the artistic practice of drama*. The programme of study lists the following statutory requirements that pupils should be taught:

- Listen and respond appropriately to adults and their peers.
- Ask relevant questions to extend their understanding and knowledge.
- Use relevant strategies to build their vocabulary.
- Articulate and justify answers, arguments and opinions.
- Give well-structured descriptions, explanations and narratives for different purposes, including for expressing feelings.
- Maintain attention and participate actively in collaborative conversations, staying on topic and initiating and responding to comments.
- Use spoken language to develop understanding through speculating, hypothesising, imagining and exploring ideas.
- Speak audibly and fluently with an increasing command of Standard English.

- Participate in discussions, presentations, performances, role play, improvisations.
- Gain, maintain and monitor the interest of the listener(s).
- Consider and evaluate different viewpoints, attending to and building on the contributions of others.
- Select and use appropriate registers for effective communication.

(DfE, 2013: 17)

The statutory requirements say that these statements *apply to all years* but should build on what has been achieved in previous years, and should be taught at an age-appropriate level.

What might this look like in school? Imagine you are visiting a school for the first time. You are trying to locate the classroom you are visiting but have misunderstood the instructions given you at reception. Two children in the corridor notice that you are lost, greet you politely and ask if they can help. They escort you to the classroom, and tell you about the school on the way. Inside the classroom, children are working in small groups. They are all contributing to the discussions, listening with interest and respect to each other but unafraid to challenge and disagree. You then attend a school assembly; pupils are giving a presentation about a recent residential trip, with a slide show they have produced, and a lively and entertaining account of some of the highlights of the trip. They speak confidently, clearly and audibly without notes. Many schools would achieve these outcomes with some pupils; the aim should be to achieve them for all by the end of the primary years. In terms of progression, it is useful to think at what age we might realistically expect most children to achieve them.

Consider the following model for expectations in speaking: it suggests that children should meet increasing demands in terms of the size and nature of the audience they are speaking to, the familiarity and complexity of the topic they are speaking about, and the effectiveness of their communication. For example, many of us are fluent and confident talking about a topic we know well to a familiar audience, but much less comfortable talking about something we do not understand very well to people we do not know.

General expectations for speaking

Age	Audience	Topic	Style
4 (possible baseline expectations)	Familiar adult Other child	Familiar topics, e.g. home life, current activity	Communicating simple information effectively and audibly
5 (end of Early Years Foundation Stage)	Unfamiliar adults Groups of children	Topics being learned about Recent events	Facing an audience, audible

Age	Audience	Topic	Style
7 (end of Key Stage 1)	Whole class Adults in more formal situations	Simple explanations Opinions	Fluent and with some confidence
11 (end of Key Stage 2)	Whole school Range of adults from outside school	Complex explanations Points of view, opinions (debates)	Formal Using visual aids effectively Varying voice to maintain interest

Of course, some children will achieve these expectations much earlier; the important point is that planning should aim to ensure that all children achieve them by the end of the relevant stage.

The programme of study does not claim to provide age-related expectations, but it is interesting to follow a strand through. Group discussion, for example, can be tracked as follows:

Year 1	Rules for effective discussions should be agreed with and demonstrated for pupils. They should be helped to develop and evaluate them, with the expectation that everyone takes part. Pupils should be helped to consider the opinions of others.
Year 2	Discussion should be demonstrated to pupils. They should be guided to participate in it and they should be helped to consider the opinion of others. They should receive feedback on their discussions.
Years 3 and 4	They should help to develop, agree on and evaluate rules for effective discussion. The expectation should be that all pupils take part.
Years 5 and 6	Participate in discussions, building on their own and others' ideas and challenging views courteously Provide reasoned justifications for their views Pupils should have guidance about and feedback on the quality of their contributions to discussions

(DfE, 2013)

While there is a sense of the start point and end point in terms of teaching, the steps in between, and particularly in terms of learning rather than teaching, are far from clear. Two aspects need to be considered – ability to follow (and formulate and evaluate) rules for discussion; and quality of contribution (for example, that it is not enough simply to state a view, but that it needs to be explained and justified). Expectations for progression might then be formulated as in the following model:

General expectations for group discussion

Age	Understanding the rules	Making contributions
4 (possible baseline expectations)	Speak when spoken to	Make an appropriate response to a question or statement
5 (end of Early Years Foundation Stage)	Take turns in discussion, supported by an adult	Make a contribution which is relevant to the topic
7 (end of Key Stage 1)	Take turns in discussion without adult support	Express ideas clearly, taking account of the contributions of others (e.g. agreeing, disagreeing, adding extra information)
11 (end of Key Stage 2)	Organise roles within the group and fulfil them effectively (e.g. managing discussion and drawing everyone in) and devise own rules (e.g. how decisions are to be reached)	Express ideas clearly and persuasively, giving reasons and evidence; respond constructively to others' contributions and accept critical comments in a positive way

The Primary National Strategy materials *Speaking, Listening, Learning: working with children in Key Stages 1 and 2* (DCSF, 2003) provide useful and detailed teaching objectives for Years 1 to 6, along with guidance on progression in the four strands of speaking, listening, group discussion and drama.

Planning for listening

With an understanding of desired outcomes and progression towards them in mind, we turn towards planning for speaking and listening, and first towards planning for listening. It may seem odd to consider this separately, but there tends to be a view that children have many opportunities to listen and therefore that there is no need to consider exactly what is involved, whether there is a progression in listening skills, and how they can be developed, other than by giving children lots of opportunities to listen. (One might argue that actually children do far too much listening in school, and not enough thinking, talking and doing.) In fact, there are different types of listening and children need to become aware of these and of which is required in different situations. First, there is the close, critical listening needed when something important is being talked about. We know that we must remember and understand what is being said and that it requires our full attention. There is a limit to how much of this any listener can do on any one occasion. Then there is a lower level monitoring of talk, sometimes described, delightfully, as 'having half an ear out'. We may do this when several conversations are going on at once, or when familiar content is being repeated. Children may listen in this way if they have already understood an explanation or instructions which are being repeated. A third aspect of listening is paying attention to non-verbal communication and the interplay between that and the language: they may be aligned, for example when 'This is very important' is accompanied by a raised index finger and a serious expression – or may contradict each other, leaving the audience to decide which is the 'real' message. For example, when 'Mrs Smith thinks this is very important', with the emphasis on 'Mrs Smith' and an accompanying a raised eyebrow and slight smile, we may infer that the speaker does not entirely share Mrs Smith's view.

There is an often-quoted ready reckoner for children's attention spans – a minute for every year of their age plus an additional minute. A minute's thought shows that this is a gross over-simplification: a four year old may be attentive for only a minute when an adult is talking about something not of interest to him, but able to concentrate for a long period when playing. However, it is important that children learn to listen for increasing periods of time, particularly as the concepts and topics they are learning about become increasingly complex. They will also need to learn to rely less on visual aids, as many abstract concepts cannot be helpfully explained visually. Even so, expectations must be realistic. If children are tired or anxious they will find it harder to listen and absorb what they are hearing. Many adults will admit that even when they are trying hard to listen to something which is important and interesting to them, after a while their attention drifts. A day of listening can feel like harder work than a day of teaching.

How do these considerations translate into planning? First, general planning needs to be reviewed to check what demands are being made on children. Are there days when every lesson has a significant element of close listening? Could lessons be sequenced so that art, music, PE, and design and technology provide a balance to more talk-based subjects? Within lessons, can content be limited to avoid the need for very lengthy introductions and explanations? Can organisation of independent work be kept simple to avoid the need for lengthy instructions? (The carousel approach, for example, can mean children having to listen to explanations for several tasks before they start work, and then finding they have forgotten those explanations as they move around.) Finally, can some silent times be planned into the school day?

A headteacher of a two-class rural school, who taught her class of 7 to 11 year olds for four and a half days a week and also supervised them at lunchtime, played music while the children (and she) ate, to provide a peaceful interlude in the middle of the day. Silence can give children thinking time, or allow them to focus fully on a task, and also free them for a short while from the heavy listening demands of the primary classroom.

Planning for speaking

Here are two scenarios that are likely to be familiar to all of us.

The Reception class is doing a Christmas play. The main part is the Christmas star. Lucy is already five, and is a confident child with a loud voice and a good memory. Morgan is a shy four and a half year old. Lucy is chosen to play the part of the star.

Thirty teachers have gathered for a training session. They are discussing a topic in groups of six. In one group, Saffron has volunteered to make notes, and has also made several useful contributions to the discussion. Gemma has been silent throughout. The session leader asks for a group member to feed back to the large group. After a moment's silence, Saffron sighs and (as usual) volunteers.

It is probably true that those who most need the practice in speaking are least likely to get it – least likely to volunteer, least likely to be chosen. Indeed, we may well see what Cunningham and Stanovich (1998) referred to in the context of reading as the 'Matthew effect' at work here, based on the Bible quotation, *For unto every one that hath shall be given, and he shall have abundance: but from him that hath not shall be taken away even that which he hath* (Matthew 25: 29, KJV). In other words, those children who are already confident and articulate talk most and in a wider range of contexts. Planning has to address this problem. Indeed, even listening may be affected by the difference in speaking opportunities, as those who do not expect to participate actively are less likely to listen carefully and critically. Was Gemma, in the example above, following the discussion and in her own mind responding and evaluating, or was she passive or even inattentive? Did other children in Lucy's class watch her and note how she spoke clearly and loudly enough to be heard by the back row of parents in the hall? Planning also has to address the difficulty that just as no play yet written has thirty good speaking parts, it is difficult to give children enough practice at speaking if this is attempted largely through individual children speaking in a whole-class context. It is worth noting, however, that choral speaking can give children good practice of speaking clearly and with expression, and it provides the same type of support which shared reading offers to early readers: no individual is in the spotlight, and the less capable can follow the lead of the more capable. It fits well with an important feature of the programme of study – learning poetry by heart. This should build on the learning of nursery rhymes and poems in the Foundation Stage, and the thread can be followed through, as in the earlier example of group discussion:

Y1:	learning to appreciate rhymes and poems and to recite some by heart
Y2:	continuing to build up a repertoire of poems learned by heart, appreciating these and reciting some, with appropriate intonation to make the meaning clear
Y3 and 4:	preparing poems and playscripts to read aloud and to perform, showing understanding through intonation, tone, volume and action
Y5 and 6:	learning a wider range of poetry by heart; preparing poems and plays to read aloud and to perform, showing understanding through intonation, tone and volume so that the meaning is clear to an audience. (DfE, 2013: 21–44)

While choral speaking gives all children opportunity to practise those speaking skills which effectively treat the voice as a musical instrument, using intonation, pitch and volume to convey meaning and emotion and to engage the audience, it does not provide them with opportunities for that other important aspect of speaking – expressing themselves fluently in their own words. It is perfectly possible to have a whole class writing at the same time, but to give every child the opportunity to talk to the whole class for just five minutes twice a week would take a quarter of the teaching time available in a week. Working within the time constraints, therefore, requires two strategies: balancing whole-class, group and paired work, and planning for speaking and listening across the curriculum.

Whole-class, group and paired work: planning for the statutory requirements

The National Curriculum programme of study states that

> pupils should be taught to develop their competence in spoken language and listening to enhance the effectiveness with which they are able to communicate across a range of contexts and to a range of audiences. They should therefore have opportunities to work in groups of different sizes – in pairs, small groups, large groups and as a whole class. (DfE, 2013: 17)

While most of the requirements can be met in any of those contexts, they may fit best in one. A useful guiding principle is that whatever can be done in paired work or group work should be mainly done in these contexts, as they offer the most regular and extensive opportunities for children to be actively engaged in talk. In the table which follows, suggesting most appropriate contexts for different aspects of speaking and listening, extracts from the National Curriculum programme of study are in italics.

Pairs	Groups	Whole class
maintain attention and participate actively in collaborative conversations, staying on topic and initiating and responding to comments	*listen and respond appropriately to adults and their peers*	*speak audibly and fluently with an increasing command of Standard English*
Children should be participating equally in paired work, rather than one partner dominating, and they should respond to each other by agreeing, extending or offering different views and ideas.	Groups of children may be talking without an adult present, but adults may be present on occasion to guide discussion and/or make assessments and give feedback on children's participation and contributions.	While children are usually audible in paired and group work, it is quite common for them not to speak loudly enough to be heard in a whole-class context, and rather than making this a clear expectation, teachers sometimes simply repeat inaudible contributions.
use spoken language to develop understanding through speculating, hypothesising, imagining and exploring ideas	*give well-structured descriptions, explanations and narratives for different purposes, including for expressing feelings*	*participate in discussions, presentations, performances, role play, improvisations and debates*
A group of five or six children may not offer the time and receptive listening needed for this type of exploratory talk.	These activities need a rather larger audience than one talk partner who may share the speaker's viewpoint and understanding.	Children do need the confidence to take part in these activities in front of the whole class.
ask relevant questions to extend their understanding and knowledge	*articulate and justify answers, arguments and opinions*	*gain, maintain and monitor the interest of the listener(s)*
Children typically ask very few questions of this kind in the classroom. Paired work offers a supportive context for generating such questions, which can then be reported back to a group or whole class.	*consider and evaluate different viewpoints, attending to and building on the contributions of others* Working in a group is likely to mean a range of views can be expressed, and there is more need to explain and justify points of view.	In paired work and group work, listeners feel more constrained to pay attention since inattention is obvious. The challenge comes in maintaining the attention of a larger group, as teachers are only too well aware.

select and use appropriate registers for effective communication

The register appropriate to paired work may be different from that appropriate to talk in the whole-class context, depending on the purpose of the talk and the relationship between the pair.

use relevant strategies to build their vocabulary

While children are most likely to encounter new vocabulary in the whole-class context, they may prefer to try it out in a less public arena.

Cross-curricular planning

Rather than produce a separate plan for speaking and listening, a practical approach is to review the medium-term plans for the term or half term for all subjects, and identify meaningful opportunities for speaking and listening within them. Could some drama be built into the history plan? Does the geography topic lend itself to a formal debate? Does the class novel chosen for English have themes that lend themselves to group discussion? These identified opportunities then become lessons in which speaking and listening is explicitly planned for, with clear learning outcomes and success criteria. This approach fits well with the move towards a cross-curricular approach to planning in many schools. Below is an example of how this might work during the course of a half term.

Subject	Speaking and listening opportunity
English: fiction	Debate on a moral or social issue
Mathematics: solving simple number problems	Individual children explain to their group how they have solved a problem
Science: shadow investigation	Groups report back to whole class on their findings
History: the Romans in Britain	Drama – hot-seat kings of British tribes during the invasion; forum theatre – building of Hadrian's wall
Geography: land use – local area	Group presentations on different land uses, e.g. dairy farming, arable farming, moorland
Design and technology	Group discussion to develop brief for carrier bag design

Once the overview has been produced, it is essential that planning moves from simply providing opportunities to considering the class's level of attainment in the relevant aspect of speaking and listening, and therefore what the focus of teaching might be. For example, it may have been noted in group discussions that many of the children tend to make assertions or express views without giving reasons or justification. The groups for the design and technology activity might be organised with a leader, whose responsibility it is to ensure that all members express a view, and a scribe, who records the views and the reasons given. The group could then check that all members have supported their view with at least one reason, and then evaluate the different ideas and make a decision – for example, on what materials to use.

Assessing speaking and listening

> Pupils should receive constructive feedback on their spoken language and listening, not only to improve their knowledge and skills but also to establish secure foundations for effective spoken language in their studies at primary school, helping them to achieve in secondary education and beyond. (DfE, 2013: 18)

As with any area of learning, assessment and feedback should be focused on the learning objectives, and should be specific, giving a clear indication of how to improve. In order to measure progress, it is important to assess at the beginning as well as the end of a teaching sequence or intervention. The following case study shows how this can work in the context of a whole class.

Case study   Teacher assessment

George, a newly qualified teacher in a Year 5 class, felt that he spent a great deal of time repeating what children said in whole-class sessions so that the rest of the class could hear. He asked his teaching assistant to fill in a tracker showing which children's responses she could hear, sitting at the back of the class, and made sure that over the next day or so he asked questions of every child. The tracker showed that a third of the children were not generally audible. George began to ask children to repeat what they had said rather than doing it for them. He also explained the importance of making sure that everyone could hear what was said, and experimented with a horse-shoe arrangement of tables so the children could all see each other. A reassessment after a few weeks found that all but one of the class was now generally audible, without the need for reminders.

George also noticed that in some groups, discussion was dominated by one or two members. He used a simple proforma to record how many contributions to discussion each member of the group made, and whether they were long (several sentences) or short (a few words). He shared his assessments with the groups and prompted a discussion about why some children talked much more than others, and what could be done about it. The groups then generated their own rules for discussion, and a class list was drawn up. At the beginning of each group discussion time over the next month, George asked a different group to recall as many of the rules as they could. At the end of the month, he reassessed to check whether children were playing a more equal part, and fed this back to them.

While it is true that constructive feedback is essential, it is important to note that it does not have to come only from the teacher: peer assessment has an important role to play, and even more important, self-assessment. If children are able to reflect thoughtfully and honestly on their own speaking and listening skills, they are likely to be able to improve them. Video recording of presentations, debates and discussions gives children an opportunity to see themselves as others see them, to have time for real reflection on their performance, to discuss with others, and to assess themselves against shared criteria. This is not something that can be done very often, however, so it is important that children learn to self-assess in a meaningful way.

Case study   Developing self-assessment

Emily, a PGCE trainee in a Year 3 class, wanted to develop children's self-assessment of their speaking and listening skills. She introduced a 'thumbs up' system at the end of lessons where there had been a speaking and listening learning objective, but felt that the children were not really thinking about their own attainment in any depth. She then tried a checklist of the success criteria for the children to complete, but again found that they tended to tick all the criteria without any real thought. Emily began to wonder if the children really understood how to reflect on their performance, and so she modelled reflecting on her own lesson introduction, and on whether she had given a clear explanation of the concept she was teaching and whether her instructions for the task were easy to follow. She asked children to share their reflections on their own speaking and listening with a partner, and found that her modelling and the paired reflection produced more thoughtful and accurate self-assessment, with children discussing the evidence for each criterion before reaching a judgement, and being prepared to say that they had not been successful on all criteria.

Teacher assessment of speaking and listening should be manageable and purposeful. There is no point making long and detailed individual assessments if they do not inform planning and teaching. There is also a danger that if lengthy checklists are completed for each child, judgements are made in haste without the evidence to support them. Decisions need to be made as to whether assessments need to be made of all children, or whether assessment of a sample of the class would provide enough information to inform planning. Checklists can be useful when used to provide a range of possible areas to assess, rather than for individual records. (The statutory requirements listed at the beginning of the chapter could be used in this way.) For example, a checklist might suggest assessing whether children ask questions. The statutory requirements state that children should *ask relevant questions to extend their understanding and knowledge* (DfE, 2013: 17). What does this really mean? First, we would presumably set aside simple procedural questions.

The significance of asking questions is surely that it indicates engagement with the topic being talked about and a level of confidence in engaging in the discussion. But we might have to listen to many hours of discussions to happen to catch every child in the class spontaneously asking enough questions to say that they had achieved that outcome. If we try to manage the assessment by asking all children to generate questions about a particular topic, it may well be that some of them would never in normal circumstances ask questions. However, if we observe one or two group discussions and note any questions asked, we should have a picture of whether all, most, some or none of the children ask questions, and whether those questions do extend understanding and knowledge. In contrast, the requirement for children to *participate actively in collaborative conversations* (DfE, 2013: 17) could be assessed quickly for all children in, for example, an ICT lesson, by pairing the children up at the computers in an ICT suite, and then scanning the class two or three times to check whether the children are simply taking turns at the task or whether they are discussing it as they work.

Final thoughts...

As Chapter 1 concluded, good subject knowledge is crucial to effective teaching. Without a good understanding of the skills involved in speaking and listening and how they develop, planning and assessment will not be purposeful and effective. With that understanding, neither assessment nor planning should be burdensome or complicated.

References

Brien, J. (2012) *Teaching Primary English*. London: Sage.

Cunningham, A.E. and Stanovich, K.E. (1998) What reading does for the mind. *American Educator,* 2: 8–17.

DCSF (2003) *Speaking, Listening. Learning: working with children in Key Stages 1 and 2*. London: DCSF.

DfE (2013) *The National Curriculum in England: Key Stages 1 and 2 Framework Document*. London: DfE.

CHAPTER 7

CHALLENGES: CHILDREN'S COMMUNICATION DIFFICULTIES

Department for Education (2014) statistics on special educational needs show that speech language and communication needs (SLCN), along with emotional and behavioural difficulties, are the most common type of special needs seen in schools. Yet they are sometimes described as a 'hidden disability', less easy to identify than other needs. There is a wide range of different speech, language and communication needs, from the child who does not speak at all to the child whose speech is almost impossible to understand, to the child who talks freely but does not seem to understand the social conventions of talk and who therefore may appear rude and find it difficult to develop relationships with others. These needs may be mild or severe, transitory or long lasting. Although they may not be obvious, SLCN can have a huge impact on children's learning and development, as so much learning is language-based. They also often affect children's well-being, and lead to behaviour, learning and emotional difficulties (Bercow, 2008). This link between language needs and social, emotional and behavioural difficulties can work in both directions: it may be that communication difficulties result in children becoming frustrated or isolated, or it may be that emotional difficulties are a cause of language difficulties, as with selective mutism, where children who are able to talk quite freely in some situations, typically at home, are persistently silent in other contexts.

The impact of communication difficulties

A report from the children's communication charity I CAN, *The Cost to the Nation of Children's Poor Communication*, published in 2006, suggested that speech, language and communication difficulties had a negative impact not only on children themselves but also on their families and the nation as a whole. While the cost to individuals was in terms of lower educational attainment and emotional, behavioural and social difficulties, and poorer employment opportunities, parents reported increased emotional and financial difficulties as a result of their children's unmet language needs. For the nation there were the increased financial costs of special education provision, the cost implications of poorer employment prospects, and additional social costs in terms of criminal justice system costs and mental health issues. The report called for much more effective early intervention and predicted that this would be highly cost effective, as the Perry Pre-School Programme (High Scope) had proved to be in the United States (Lynch, 2005).

When children begin school, about 5 to 7 per cent are likely to have significant difficulties with speech and language, and for about one in a hundred these difficulties are likely to require specialist support (I CAN, 2006). Children from disadvantaged backgrounds are more likely to have speech, language and communication difficulties: researchers for Save the Children's *Read On. Get On* campaign (2014) analysed the National Pupil Database in a longitudinal study of 19,000 children, and found that four out of ten of the poorest boys were at least 15 months behind in language development at the end of the Early Years Foundation Stage, while 27 per cent of the poorest girls were also not meeting expected levels. The National Literacy Trust (2005) reported a number of surveys showing that a majority of headteachers, teachers and nursery workers felt that increasing numbers of young children had SLCN, but there is as yet no conclusive evidence that this is the case, and it could be that early years practitioners are simply more aware of the importance of early identification and intervention.

What is meant by speech, language and communication?

The terms 'speech', 'language' and 'communication' have specific meanings in the educational context and among health professionals. Speech refers to producing the sounds of the language (the phonology strand encountered in Chapter 1), while language refers more widely to the strands of vocabulary and syntax (structuring language) and communication to pragmatics (using language in different contexts). Non-verbal communication – expression, gesture – supports verbal communication. It is important to note that there are other ways of communicating, known as *augmentative and alternative communication* (AAC), which support or substitute for oral language. These include the use of signs and symbols, including systems such as British Sign Language (BSL), which is a language in its own right, and Makaton, which uses some signs taken from BSL and which is used alongside spoken language, and voice output communication aids.

Communication and language difficulties can broadly be categorised as *receptive* (to do with hearing and understanding language) or *expressive* (to do with producing words and sentences and using language).

Receptive language difficulties

Receptive difficulties are often less easy to identify than expressive difficulties. Children with receptive difficulties may be perceived as being inattentive, unco-operative, difficult, shy, passive or lacking in motivation, rather than as having language difficulties. They may also been seen as 'low ability' or having more general developmental delay, and their non-verbal skills may be underestimated. There is a range of receptive difficulties. Children may have a permanent or temporary hearing impairment, ranging from mild to severe, and there may be particular difficulties in the classroom context, if for example there is a high level of background noise, or the speaker is softly spoken or does not articulate clearly, or when they cannot see the speaker's face. Glue ear and even heavy colds can affect hearing on a temporary basis. In contrast, children may hear perfectly well but have problems with listening and attention, for example not tuning in when they are being spoken to, being unable to listen while they are doing something, and needing time to process what is said to them before they can respond appropriately. Processing difficulties can be intensified when there is a great deal of language to listen to, or speakers talk very fast, or use unfamiliar vocabulary or complex grammatical structures such as passive sentences (for example, *The dog was attacked by the seagull* rather than *The seagull attacked the dog*). Negatives can also be confusing, as in 'Bring me all the ones which haven't been opened' or 'If you haven't finished yet go to the table by the window'. Older children may also find it more difficult to remember what they have heard than what they have read, as they cannot process at their own pace or return to problematic points.

Comprehension difficulties can also occur when children need to make inferences about what they hear. A limited vocabulary can have a significant impact on children's comprehension, leading to misunderstandings and incomplete understanding or at times even a complete breakdown of comprehension. Beyond this, as children grow older it is assumed that they will be able to 'read between the lines' of what is said to them, making connections and drawing on their knowledge of the world. For some children, this is an unwise assumption to make. Consider the following example, where a Year 5 teacher, telling the story of Noah's Ark, tries to illustrate how heavy the rain must have been by reference to an experience of his own.

> *About three years ago in the Pyrenees when we were climbing we were camped right on top of one of the mountains at three thousand metres, and we bivouacked for the night, and unfortunately we picked a bad night for doing it.*

The listeners may not know what or where the Pyrenees are; there are clues later in the sentence with the references to mountains and climbing, but even so making the inference from these would depend on knowing that people go rock-climbing in mountains. Bivouacked is unlikely to be understood by many 10 year olds, and unusually one of the class did ask what it meant. A child who regularly went hill-climbing would appreciate that mountains three thousand metres high are far bigger than any in this country, but most children would be unlikely to make this inference and realise the potential dangers of camping at that height. The most basic inference which the listener needs to make, though, is that *we* refers to the teacher and his family or friends, rather than the class; he does not make this explicit.

Idiomatic language, where intended meaning is not immediately obvious, may pose particular comprehension problems: expressions such as 'It's on the tip of my tongue', 'A rags to riches story', or 'She came to a sticky end' can be baffling to a child who is not familiar with them. Receptive difficulties may be even harder to identify when children have developed strategies for coping: for example, copying others rather than following instructions. Adults assume understanding of the language and therefore appropriate support is not given.

Case study   Receptive language difficulties

Stefan, aged 7, was a lively child with interests which at times bordered on obsessions. He talked fluently and at great length about subjects which interested him, and had a wide vocabulary. However, he found it difficult to engage in conversation and to respond appropriately in social situations; he also found group discussion challenging, and would shout out comments in the whole-class situation and interrupt other children in small group talk, seeming to find it hard to listen to others and respond to their contributions. He became distressed at attempts to control his interruptions and desire at times to monopolise discussion, and other children were increasingly reluctant to work with him. His class teacher addressed Stefan's needs by seating him whenever possible with a teaching assistant during whole-class sessions, and allowing him to address his comments quietly to her; she also worked on social language such as greetings, apologies and saying thank you in role-play activities with Stefan, as did his parents. The class teacher monitored and managed his participation in small group discussions and ensured he was placed with different children rather than always in the same group.

Expressive language difficulties

Children with expressive difficulties, who find it hard to communicate successfully, may become frustrated and angry or may withdraw and become passive. They may appear rude if they have difficulties with the social aspects of language. The range of expressive difficulties parallels the range of receptive difficulties. Children may have difficulties with articulation – the production of speech sounds because of physical/motor difficulties.

Case study   Problems with consonant sounds

Julia's language developed well in her early years, and by three she had an extensive vocabulary and combined words to express a wide range of ideas and views. However, at three and a half she had difficulty producing many consonant sounds and all consonant clusters, with the result that often not even her parents could understand her. She found this intensely frustrating. At four she was referred to a speech and language therapist for help with the sounds she still could not produce - /s/, /sh/, /ch/, /t/ and /j/ – the last meaning that she could not pronounce her own name. Her parents and teacher followed the programme planned for her by the speech and language therapist, and after four months she had mastered most of the sounds she had previously been unable to produce. Although she often needed reminders, her speech was much clearer and she settled in school and began to make friends.

More commonly, development of the phonological system (the system of sounds in words) is delayed or disordered, so children may be able to articulate a sound in isolation but cannot produce particular combinations of sounds, or sequence sounds correctly in words (for example, saying *aminal* for *animal* or *hostapul* for *hospital*). As Chapter 1 showed, these organisational difficulties are typical of young children, but in some children they continue beyond the early years. Phonological problems when severe may mean that much of what the child says cannot be understood, even by family, friends and teachers, and this can have both emotional and social consequences. It should be noted that some mispronunciations may result from children not hearing words correctly (for example, saying *windowsilve* for *windowsill*).

There may also be difficulties with fluency. All informal speech includes what are known as normal non-fluency features, such as hesitations, use of fillers such as *um* and *like*, repetitions and false starts such as *Can I – I mean, is it all right if...*

However, some children's speech is markedly less fluent than that of other children of the same age, and this can make children self-conscious and demand patience from listeners. Stammering, also known as stuttering, is a difficulty with fluency, in which the speaker repeats a word or sound, or prolongs a sound, or the sound does not come out at all. Stammering usually starts between the ages of two and five, and is more common in boys; four out of five children who stammer will eventually achieve normal fluency, even if they receive no support. It may be affected by context and factors such as tiredness or mood. Stammering can affect children's confidence and self-image, and therapy for older children may focus on these issues more than on developing fluency; early intervention is more effective in reducing stammering. The memorable film *The King's Speech* highlighted the difficulties faced by adults who stammer, showing how George VI, unexpectedly thrust into the limelight by his brother's abdication, battled with his stammer with the help of a therapist.

Expressive language difficulties may also include vocabulary difficulties, either because the child's vocabulary is extremely limited or because there are difficulties in finding the right word. Children may cope with this by substituting easier words or catch-all words such as *thingummy*, but this can restrict their ability to show what they have learned or communicate their ideas and views. There may also be difficulties in following grammatical rules such as those governing tense. Of course, it is important to distinguish between this and dialect forms or those typically used by young children. A major area of difficulty with expressive language is the skill of social communication: children may find it hard to start conversations and keep them going, to understand the 'rules' of talk, or to see others' point of view and to alter their language depending on the social situation. In the wider area of communication, they may find it difficult to use eye contact and gesture appropriately. They are often seen as rude or odd as a consequence, and these difficulties are likely to affect relationships and social development. It is worth noting that the Communication Trust (2011) states that all children with autistic spectrum disorders have SLCN. Expressive language difficulties may also have an impact on learning, if children struggle to ask questions, reason and problem-solve, and monitor and evaluate their own language.

Case study   Expressive language difficulties – selective mutism?

Lisa, a bilingual Year 2 pupil from a Hong Kong Chinese background, had not spoken in class since she began school two years earlier. She nodded and shook her head in response to questions, and was sometimes observed speaking to a friend at playtime, but did not speak either in the whole-class context, in small groups or in a one-to-one situation with her teacher. Her attainment in literacy and mathematics was good. She did read her reading book to adults, but was barely audible. Her parents reported that she spoke freely at home, and they were reluctant to have her referred to a speech and language therapist, as they felt she was making good progress academically and would in time develop enough confidence to speak in class. Her teacher continued to talk to her, and to facilitate non-verbal responses, while building in paired talk opportunities during which Lisa sat at the back of the carpet area, to give her a degree of privacy, with the child she spoke to at playtime.

Selective mutism can be seen primarily as an anxiety disorder, and educational psychologists or other services may have a key role as well as or rather than speech and language therapists. It is important to note that bilingual children, children whose language development is delayed, and children who simply are quiet, may speak little or not at all in some situations, and that it would not be appropriate to jump to a diagnosis of selective mutism.

Primary and secondary language and communication needs

A different way of looking at SLCN is to view them as being either *primary*, where marked difficulties occur without any other developmental difficulties, or *secondary*, where they are associated with other needs such as cerebral palsy or hearing loss (Bercow, 2008). The Communication Trust (2011) points out that all children with autistic spectrum disorders and all children with learning difficulties have SLCN.

Language delay or language disorder?

These terms are sometimes used interchangeably, and the term specific language impairment is also sometimes used, but there is an important distinction between developmental language delay and developmental language disorder. Where language development is delayed it may start significantly later than usual, and/or be much slower than normal, but it follows the same pattern and sequence as is typical of most children. Less commonly, language develops in a different order or unusual mistakes are made, unlike the typical mistakes of normal language development, and this is described as a language disorder. Disorders may be very varied in nature and severity, and where there is a disorder, language development is also likely to be delayed. There are many risk factors associated with SLCN. About a third of children with such needs have a close family member with similar difficulties. Low birth weight or preterm birth doubles the risk of language difficulties, as do delayed motor skills such as walking, throwing and catching balls, and drawing. SLCN are two to three times more common in boys than in girls (Afasic n.d.). Knowing these factors, however, does not mean that the causes of language difficulties are known, and the priority is early identification and support (DCSF, 2008).

Identifying and supporting children with SLCN

One of the key messages of the Bercow Report (2008) was the importance of early identification in order that appropriate support can be given and the risks of lower attainment, emotional and social difficulties, mental health issues, and poorer employment prospects be avoided. The report suggested that the majority of SLCN are apparent from the second year of life, though some may only emerge quite late in the child's education, as the language demands of the school curriculum become more complex. Bercow notes that it can be particularly difficult to identify a developmental language disorder where children's early language environment has been impoverished. An effective partnership with parents is clearly essential here, both to gain a sense of how able they are to support their children's early language development, and also, importantly, to gain the parents' views on their children's language. Sometimes parents are very aware that one of their children seems to be starting to talk much later than another, or that development is much slower. They may, of course, describe a child unrecognisable to the early years teacher, who never stops talking at home, asks endless questions and has a wide vocabulary.

Bercow points out the increased difficulty of identifying language difficulties when children are learning English as an additional language, as a level of delay is normal when children are not only learning two words for everything but also getting to grips with the different grammars of the two or more languages they are learning. Secondary speech and language difficulties, which are associated with disabilities such as Down's Syndrome, cerebral palsy, autistic spectrum disorder, learning difficulties or hearing impairment, are probably more likely to be identified than SLCN which occur in isolation.

Tracking of language development is essential for identification of children in need of support. Schools may also decide to screen some or all pupils, using screening tools such as the Universally Speaking checklists from the Communication Trust (2011), Gross (2013), the National Strategies' Inclusion Development Programme (2008), or I CAN's primary milestones document. However, it is the teacher's responsibility to notice children who are struggling with their communication; while some may have already been identified by health visitors, parents or early years workers, others will have slipped through the net. Knowing what to expect at different ages and stages is important here, and Chapters 1 and 6 provide guidance with this. Teachers are not on their own in this, though: the school SENCO is likely to be the first professional to contact where there are concerns, and speech and language therapists, educational psychologists and specialist or advisory teachers may be able to offer advice and support, and of course working with parents is paramount.

Identification does not necessarily mean labelling. It is more important to be clear about the nature and impact of the child's difficulties and how to support them than to have a 'diagnosis'. Having said this, for some children it can be a relief to feel that there is a reason for their difficulties and they are not somehow at fault, and some families also find it helpful in terms of understanding their children's needs better. The key is to remember that support needs to be matched to the individual child's needs rather than the label.

The three waves model of support

The three waves of intervention model first introduced by the Primary National Strategy (DfES, 2006) is a useful way of looking at support for children with SLCN. It matches the three levels of support recommended by the Better Communication Research Programme (Lindsay et al., 2012), which proposed universal, targeted and specialist support to meet different levels of need.

Wave 1 is 'quality first teaching' – in other words, providing a rich language environment for all children, with a clear focus on effective classroom communication and on developing children's language skills. This has been discussed in the previous chapters, but it must be emphasised that without it additional support is unlikely to be successful. It is also important to say that Wave 1 includes differentiated teaching and support, to meet the needs of all learners, and that considering the needs of children with language difficulties is actually likely to be beneficial for all children. Wave 1 support will be considered in more detail later in the chapter.

Wave 2 consists of interventions for children who need additional support to help them to meet age-related expectations. These are likely to be small group interventions, led by appropriately trained teaching assistants, time-limited (e.g. for a term or a year). There are increasing numbers of such language programmes, some of which have been evaluated rigorously and have shown good evidence of impact. Examples of these are *Language4Reading*, now called the Nuffield Early Language Intervention, for the Early Years Foundation Stage, developed by the University of York, and I CAN; *Talk Boost*, a 10-week programme for Reception and Key Stage 1, with training and resources provided by I CAN; *talkingpartners@primary* from Education Works for children aged 4 to 11. The Better Communication Research Programme (Law et al., 2012), which was part of the response to the Bercow Report, evaluated 57 intervention programmes, and the Communication Trust website provides updates on this information. As with all interventions, it is essential that staff have a good understanding of the subject and are fully trained for the specific intervention programme, and that their work is monitored and children's progress rigorously tracked so that the intervention's effectiveness can be monitored.

Wave 3 encompasses provision for a more significant and long-term level of need. It is likely to involve individual support and will require advice and support from experts such as speech and language therapists. It requires effective partnership between these specialists, school staff and parents, and additional training for school staff. Wave 3 provision may involve teaching assistant support within the class. It is important that the teaching assistant has good knowledge of language development and how to support it effectively. Blatchford et al. (2012) found that teachers tend to use 'opening up' language, encouraging talk, while teaching assistants tend to use 'closing down' strategies. Teaching assistants also usually correct mistakes, while teachers are more likely to use mistakes and misconceptions as learning opportunities – providing much richer opportunities for language. This is, of course, the broad picture and it is important to recognise that teachers too may 'close down' talk, while some teaching assistants may be very skilled at encouraging and developing talk. Wave 3 support may also involve technological support and use of signs and symbols (alternative/augmentative communication), which substitute for, or supplement oral language. Devices include high-tech aids such as computers with, for example, a single switch for children with very limited movement, or stored phrases and words which can be accessed with a single key press, and perhaps a voice. Low-tech aids include pointing boards and frames. Symbol systems may use picture symbols or abstract symbols which can be pointed to, and signing systems include simple systems such as Makaton and complex systems such as British Sign Language (BSL).

Providing an inclusive environment for communication

Wave 1 provision means not only a developing a rich language environment but also ensuring it includes all learners, including those with SLCN. The Better Communication Research Programme (Dockrell et al., 2013) produced a Communication Supporting Classrooms Observation Tool for monitoring the language learning environment, language learning opportunities and language learning interactions. Of these three aspects, high quality interactions are the most difficult to achieve – these, and language learning opportunities, have been discussed in previous chapters. A supportive environment can include strategies such as the use of visual support. Visual timetables, picture or symbols to label equipment and areas of the classroom, carefully planned displays, and visual aids in teaching will benefit all children. However, too much visual distraction can be unhelpful for some children. Reducing noise levels helps all children to focus on language. Very clear routines are also useful, with consistent ways of introducing and ending lessons, and consistency in relation to how children gain attention – *are hands up allowed but not always responded to?*, for example – and how turn-taking is managed. This does not mean routines have to be the same all the time, but if a different approach is being used then this has to be explicitly explained. Adult talk needs to be carefully reviewed and managed, and there need to be regular checks of whether children have understood. Children need to be given time to process what they hear and consider their responses (thinking time). The environment must encourage and support interaction with peers, and children also need to be given regular opportunities to reflect on their own understanding and communication. The Hanen Centre, a Canadian organisation, provides a number of evidence-based practical training programmes for early years teachers, parents and speech and language therapists.

Improving teaching and learning for children with SLCN

An important goal for all pupils is independence. For children with SLCN, this may involve improving their speech, language and communication, but also developing strategies to help them manage the linguistic demands of the classroom. There is always a danger that children with additional needs become over-dependent on the extra support they receive. While it is essential to provide support so children have full access to learning opportunities, that support should also be focused on enabling them to manage without it, if possible. Part of that move towards independence should involve giving children control over their own learning: for example, it is important, wherever possible, to include children themselves in the process of target setting and deciding how to meet their targets. They need to be encouraged to reflect on their own language learning regularly and to think about what works for them.

When teaching a class that includes children with SLCN, it is best to plan for the whole class first and only then introduce personalised strategies. Much good practice involves classroom management and routines – for example, checking where the child sits to ensure he or she can see and hear well, and ensuring that visual distractions are reduced and sound levels are low. It makes sense to seat the child with another child or children who can provide a good language model and who have the social skills to support the child with SLCN effectively. Individual aids such as symbol cards may need to be provided, and used consistently and unobtrusively. It may be necessary to make more checks on the child's understanding and progress.

It is helpful, too, for the child to receive additional feedback on their language and communication. We must also be honest if we cannot understand what the child is saying. As Chapter 1 suggested, when talking with young children, the best approach in such circumstances is to start by repeating any parts we have understood, as a check and to avoid making them repeat everything, and then ask the child to repeat the part which has not been understood: for example, 'You went somewhere with your dad, but can you just tell me *where* you went again, please?' If that is not successful, it is best to ask them to try to find a different way of saying it or showing what they mean. It is also helpful to the child to acknowledge their frustration. It is important that we respond to what they are trying to communicate rather than how they do it: when a child has made a huge effort to communicate something, nothing can be more crushing than an adult response which focuses on grammar or pronunciation (see Chapter 8). With children who stammer it is crucial to remain calm, maintain eye contact, give them as much time as they need, and not be tempted to finish off their sentence unless they indicate they would like you to. It is also helpful not to put them under pressure to speak or read aloud, but to discuss with them what they feel comfortable with. Some children, of course, may be keen to do this, despite enormous difficulties, and this enthusiasm and confidence should be welcomed.

Differentiation to meet the needs of children with SLCN may include providing alternative input, such as visual instructions instead of or alongside oral instructions; adapting tasks by, for example, breaking them down into smaller steps, offering alternative ways of recording learning, or placing individual targets on the table as a reminder. They are in danger of missing a great deal of what goes on in the classroom: by trying to see each lesson from their point of view, we are more likely to be able to make sure that they do not.

Social aspects of communication may need to be very explicitly and systematically taught. For example, children may need modelling and clear instruction on how to 'read' non-verbal communication, how to make eye contact and use gesture appropriately, how to initiate and maintain conversations, how to take turns in talk, or how to interrupt a conversation politely. Observing and discussing the emotions, behaviour and communication of others can be useful – for example, in fiction, in film or in role play and drama.

Case study   Montessori's exercises of practical life

Maria Montessori, born in 1870, was the first woman doctor in Italy, and a social reformer who became interested in the education first of children with learning difficulties, who had been considered ineducable, and then children in the slums of Rome. Part of her approach to Early Years education included lessons in 'grace and courtesy', providing children with social skills which gave them confidence because they knew how to behave and what to say in a range of common social situations, such as greeting people and saying goodbye to them, introducing themselves or others, inviting someone in, buying something in a shop, requesting something, saying please and thank you, apologising, and interrupting in an acceptable way. Of course, many parents spend a great deal of time teaching these social skills to their children, and many children seem to pick them up naturally and easily, but this does not always happen. Montessori saw these skills as part of the learning programme. In a Montessori setting the adult might begin by demonstrating, for example, an unacceptable way of interrupting a conversation, to engage and amuse the children, and then model how to interrupt politely. Children would then role-play the situation until they were confident with the communication skills involved. For children with communication difficulties these simple interactions may need systematic teaching, as the Montessori approach exemplified.

Beside the basic social skills described in the case study, children with SLCN may need careful and regular instruction in more sophisticated social skills such as negotiating with others and resolving conflicts. The teaching process of modelling, explaining, and then supporting the child in role play, may need to be to repeated many times before the skill is likely to be applied independently in real-life situations.

Final thoughts...

The Communication Trust (2011) argues that speech, language and communication difficulties do not have to be disabling for children, if adults at school and at home understand and can meet their needs. In order to be confident that you are able to do this effectively, it is helpful to establish your current level of understanding. A useful way of doing this is to complete the Speech, Language and Communication Framework self-evaluation, available from www.talkingpoint.org.uk/slcf. To improve your understanding of SLCN and how to address needs successfully, the Bercow Report (2008) recommended training such as the National Strategies' Inclusion Development Programme for speech, language and communication needs.

References

Afasic (n.d.) *What Causes Speech, Language and Communication Needs*. [Internet]. Available from: www.afasic.org.uk/recognising-a-problem/what-causes-slcn/

Bercow, J. (2008) *The Bercow Report: A Review of Services for Children and Young People (0-19) with Speech, Language and Communication Needs*. Nottingham: DCSF Publications.

Blatchford, P., Russell, A. and Webster, R. (2012) *Reassessing the Impact of Teaching Assistants: how research challenges practice and policy*. London: Routledge.

The Communication Trust (2011) *Don't Get Me Wrong*. London: The Communication Trust.

DCSF (2008) *The National Strategies Inclusion Development Programme: Speech, Language and Communication Needs*. London: DCSF.

DfE (2014) *Statistical Release: Children with Special Educational Needs 2014: An Analysis*. London: DfE.

DfES (2006) *Primary National Strategy: Leading on Intervention*. London: DfES.

Dockrell, J.E., Bakopoulou, I., Law, J., Spencer, S. and Lindsay, G. (2013) *Communication Supporting Classroom Observation Tool*. London: The Communication Trust.

Gross, J. (2013) *Time to Talk: implementing outstanding practice in speech, language and communication*. Abingdon: Routledge.

I CAN (2006) *The Cost to the Nation of Children's Poor Communication*. London: I CAN.

Law, J., Lee, W., Roulstone, S., Wren, Y., Zeng, B. and Lindsay, G. (2012) *'What Works': interventions for children and young people with speech, language and communication needs*. London: DfE.

Lindsay, G., Dockrell, J., Law, J. and Roulstone, S. (2012) *The Better Communication Research Programme: improving provision for children and young people with speech, language and communication needs*. London: DfE.

Lynch, R.G. (2005) *Early Childhood Investment: yields big payoff*. San Francisco: WestEd.

National Literacy Trust (2005) *Why Do Many Young Children Lack Basic Language Skills?* London: National Literacy Trust.
Save the Children (2014) *Read On. Get On*. London: Save the Children.

Useful websites

Afasic (charity supporting children with SLCN and their parents) www.afasic.org.uk
The Communication Trust (group of not-for-profit organisations working for children with SLCN) www.thecommunicationtrust.org.uk
Hanen Centre: www.hanen.org
I CAN (children's communication charity) www.ican.org.uk

CHAPTER 8

LANGUAGE VARIATION

Jimmy: Hey Miss, how is it yous talk so posh?
Rosemary: Actually, I don't talk posh, Jimmy. It's just that I come
            from Surrey in the south of England and so I have a
            Surrey accent, and you come from Glasgow so you have
            a Glasgow accent.
            [Jimmy thinks for a while]
Jimmy: Miss, if ah went doon where yous live, would they think
            ah talked posh?

The exchange above actually happened when a young student was volunteering in a Glasgow school. The perception that a southern English accent and dialect is 'posh' is interesting and probably accords with what much of the population would feel. The notion that having a different way of speaking from those around you might be regarded as 'posh' is intriguing. Accents and dialects have different statuses for many people and can have an impact on both our social lives and our career prospects. People have favourite accents, and accents which they dislike. Informal surveys of student teachers over many years consistently reveal that Irish, north-eastern English and lowland Scottish accents are the most popular, and Birmingham and 'cockney' accents least popular. Of course, it is ridiculous to talk of an Irish, Scottish or Midland accent, as there are great varieties of accents spoken in each area, but people tend to make generalisations and value judgements.

Many of us can also 'do accents', in that we can make passable imitations of the way people speak in different areas. We tend to do this by using trigger words and phrases which help us to get into the swing of the accent, for example:

- *Och aye* for Scottish;
- *Why aye* for north-eastern;
- *Top of the morning to you* for Irish.

It should, of course, be remembered that there are many different Scottish, Irish and north-eastern accents and dialects and that the phrases above are not used by all people in those areas.

We can also imitate dialects and know words and phrases which are used by different people, for example: *canny* and *bonny lad* in parts of the north-east; *hey up* and *nowt* in parts of the north; and *leave it out* and *you're having a laugh* in parts of the south-east. Television has opened up our knowledge of dialect and accent, and made us more aware of ways in which people speak in different areas.

Why is this relevant to what happens in schools? Most children are aware that people speak in different ways in different circumstances. They almost always know, for example, that some language which they use when playing with friends is not acceptable in the classroom. They can impersonate adults being cross or affectionate, and they copy the words and phrases their parents and teachers use.

Brien (2012: 21) describes the way in which children imitate teachers and understand different registers when playing:

> One of the most startling rites of passage for most primary teachers is when they first overhear children playing schools. What is said in the classroom will be echoed in the playground; every linguistic whim or nuance is copied for

the reason that the teacher does a lot of talking and is a very important role model in children's lives.

So children are generally aware of different ways of speaking and can even imitate these, but they also need to understand when it is acceptable (and unacceptable) to use different forms of language. This means that they need to know about dialects and accents and language registers.

Dialect and accent

These are explained in more detail below, but Crystal and Crystal's succinct definition provides a very good starting point:

> An accent is a person's distinctive pronunciation. A dialect is a much broader notion: it refers to the distinctive vocabulary and grammar of someone's use of language. If you say *eether* and I say *iyther*, that's accent. We use the same word but pronounce it differently. But if you say *I've got a new dustbin* and I say *I've gotten a new garbage can,* that's dialect. We're using different words and sentence patterns to talk about the same thing. (Crystal and Crystal, 2014: 15)

Dialect

The distinctive vocabulary and grammatical forms that denote different dialects usually vary between regions. However, there are also variations determined by age and social class, so that sometimes older people will continue to use dialect words and phrases which younger people tend not to use. Equally, people from different social groupings and those who have different educational backgrounds may use words and phrases that others would avoid.

For example, terms of affection vary in different dialects and include *love, duck, pet, darling, but, butty, pal* and *mate.* Sometimes it is only when we go and live somewhere else that we realise that some of the words and phrases we use are not common parlance. Students in their first weeks at university frequently discuss the variations in dialect they encounter.

Dialects generally have only a small number of distinctive grammatical features. Look at the examples below and note the elements of each which differ from Standard English:

- I done it missen.
- Wait while four o'clock.
- I were late for school.
- I don't want no trouble.
- He did it all be hisself.
- Do them jobs before you go out.
- I have wrote my name on it.

You could probably understand what each example meant, and 'translated' as follows:

- I did it myself.
- Wait until four o'clock.
- I was late for school.
- I don't want any trouble.
- He did it all by himself.
- Do those jobs before you go out.
- I have written my name on it.

As a teacher, however, you may need to explain the 'errors', discuss what would be a correct version and why, and show children how to write and, when appropriate, speak using Standard English. It may be helpful at this point to consider what is meant by the term Standard English. England's 2014 National Curriculum programme of study for English says that *pupils should be taught to speak clearly and convey ideas confidently using Standard English* (DfE, 2013), and the *Teachers' Standards* (2012) state that teachers must *demonstrate an understanding of and take responsibility for promoting high standards of literacy, articulacy and the correct use of Standard English*.

The requirement for teachers to promote correct use of Standard English is interesting, since it seems to imply that there might be a version of Standard English which is incorrect. Standard English refers to the version of English which is regarded as being correct and appropriate when writing and speaking in formal situations.

What is Standard English?

Standard English is one dialect of English and has grammatical features which distinguish it from others. It is often regarded as the 'correct' version of the language and is, for example, the one taught to foreigners learning English and in writing, although as Mallett (2002: 265) asserts, *it is not linguistically superior to non-standard dialects but for historical and cultural reasons it became the form used in speech and writing by people of high social and educational status*. Unlike other dialects it is not linked to a geographical area, so it can be spoken with any accent. It tends to be associated with educated speakers and is used in writing and formal situations. Standard English tends to have higher social status than other dialects and although very few people use Standard English all of the time, most can switch between Standard English and the dialect of their area when appropriate.

There are different versions of Standard English in different English-speaking countries. How often has your grammar and spell checker defaulted to US English? You can also choose UK English, Australian English and so on.

Why is Standard English important?

Given that very few people adhere to Standard English all of the time, how important is it that we are all able to speak, write and understand it? Bearne (1998: 4) argues that:

> since standard English is the currency of examination and of literature, media and information texts as well as assumed as part of the writing requirements of most jobs, it is the right of every child to have access to standard forms of language.

So while we may feel that different dialects should be valued and preserved, few teachers would argue that children should not learn standard forms and should use these when appropriate in speaking and writing. Apart from anything else, Standard English provides people from all regions with a common language which everyone can understand and enables communication and understanding.

When teaching Standard English, it is helpful to bear in mind the most common non-standard usages in English:

- Formation of negatives (He ain't).
- Subject–verb agreements (They was, he is sat).
- Formation of past tense (I have fell, I done it).

It is in these areas that we tend most often to find other dialects differing from Standard English.

Accent

We all have different accents. Even though we can often tell where someone comes from as soon as we have heard them say a few words, within general regional accents there are differences between people in different areas and even different families. We can usually tell which family member or friend is calling as soon as we hear them speak because of subtle differences in the way people pronounce words. Most differences between accents relate to the way we sound vowels, so 'bus' and 'foot' tend to have the same vowel phoneme in many parts of the to North of England, but are sounded differently in parts of the South.

Regional dialects are generally spoken with regional accents, but it is possible to speak any dialect with any accent, and certainly possible to use Standard English with any accent. The BBC has been keen to have a variety of accents represented by its broadcasters, but these tend to be the more favoured ones such as Scottish, Welsh and Irish rather than those from large cities, which seem to be less favoured. However, Received Pronunciation (RP), which is used by very few people, often has a higher status and is the accent used when dictionaries provide notes on pronunciation. For a delightful example of mixing RP as used in the 1940s with a dialect associated with young speakers in London see:

http://uk.youtube.com/watch?v=lwNQf08Kxsw

People often have preferences for some accents over others and this is reflected in the siting of call centres, with companies conducting research to establish which accents people like best. Notice how often the voice at the other end of the phone when you ring a bank or utility has a lowlands Scots, Irish, north-eastern or West Yorkshire accent and how rarely one from east London or the Midlands.

Wells (1982) discriminated between accents by using single words to refer to the pronunciation of a particular group of English words. The word groups were called *lexical sets* and each has a key word to identify them. For example, the *BATH* set can be used to show how people say words such as *grass, path, fast* and, of course, *bath* in different accents. Other lexical sets include the *STRUT* vowel which occurs in words such as *bus, brother, good* and *young*; the *GOAT* vowel in words such as *no, flow, nose* and *hope*; and the *NURSE* vowel in words such as *bird, word, work, church* and *learn*. Think about how you would pronounce *bath, strut, goat* and *nurse* and then consider how people with a range of accents say the words. Think, too, about how you form opinions about people based on hearing their accents.

Accents change over time and we often modify our accents so that we fit in with the people around us. Some people do this consciously and deliberately, while others do not notice that their accent has changed until they go back to the place where they grew up and friends and family make comments. Even the Queen has modified her accent during her reign, with some vowel sounds such as the 'a' in happy changing so that she now says happy rather than 'heppy'.

Teachers do not generally 'correct' or attempt to change children's accents, but often do, as you will see later, correct dialect words and phrases. While we tend to maintain that children's accents should not be 'corrected', differences in accent can prove challenging when teaching and learning phonics. The long 'a' in words like bath (bahth) and grass (grahss) associated with the South of England attracts attention and sometimes confusion in some areas of the North, with children learning that 'a' consistently makes the short vowel sound /a/ as in mat and bad, while some of their teachers lengthen the sound for words like laugh, fast and graph. Phonics programmes tend to provide very little guidance on accent, but this is an aspect of teaching which challenges many trainees. In particular, it is vowel sounds which cause misunderstandings. Look at the words below and consider how you would pronounce them and how they might be pronounced using different accents:

path but sure hair

Student teachers at one north-eastern university reported being told by teachers to teach phonics using the local accent rather than their own, with words like *sure, pure* and *cure* being sounded as if they rhymed with *brewer* and *sewer*.

Browne (2009: 23) maintained:

> Perhaps the role of the school in relation to accents should be to counter negative attitudes to them, since these can affect self-esteem and identity. A distinctive regional accent may identify a new entrant to school as coming from a different place or as being an outsider and impede the child's acceptance as a member of the new local community.

Teachers, Browne also argues here, should discuss language with children and stress 'the need to respect one's own language and that of others'.

What can teachers do?

We might consider to what extent we should correct children's use of language. What might be the benefits and disadvantages of correcting their speech? The late Alan Stibbs produced a wonderful example of what might happen if we taught children to speak like we teach them to write:

Kid (in kitchen):	Mummy, mummy (pause) Mummy, Mummy!
Mum (in next room):	Don't repeat yourself, dear.
K:	A big cat's just comed in the window.
M:	Grammar!
K:	Now puss on stove.
M:	Don't use slang. The word is 'cat'.
K:	Now cat in frying pan.
M:	Good!
K:	Fish comed out of pan.
M:	What's the good of my correcting your speech if you take no notice?
K:	Pan falled over. Fire in pan.
M:	Not a sentence.
K:	Now fire in hanged-up clothes by chimbly.
M:	Pronunciation! The word is 'chimney'. Say it our ten times.

> K: Chimney, chimney, chimby, chimly, chimbly...Now fire in granny!
> M: Try to vary the shape of your sentences.
> K: Now granny in fire.
> M: Better! But make your speech more interesting by using more describing words.
> K: See how the pretty yellow flames lick around the frail and combustible granny, like greedy, angry tongues of hungry tigers, which seem... AAARRRGGGHHH!!!
> M: Why is this sentence not finished? Five out of ten.

(as cited in Dougill and Knott, 1988: 24).

This example is designed to make a point, but if the teacher is a model of language, imitated by children, what implications does this have for the way they speak? Given that virtually no one uses Standard English all of the time, is it reasonable to expect teachers to use it consistently? Look at the examples of teachers' language below and see: a) if there is anything which deviates from Standard English; b) if you feel the teachers need to modify their language; and c) what the correct versions should be:

> Teacher A: *What was we doing in our last lesson?*
> Teacher B: *I want to see you all sat nicely on your bums.*

Teacher A has not used a non-standard verb form to go with the subject 'we' and should have used 'were'. This is a common form in many regions, with dialects using the same part of the verb for all of the past tense versions of the verb to be: I was, you was, he was, we was, they was or I were, you were, he were, we were, they were. Although this is often heard from teachers and trainee teachers, it seldom occurs in their written work. It seems that some people are aware of the need to use Standard English in writing, but revert to local dialect in speech. It could be argued that if children hear their teachers using non-standard subject verb agreements they are likely to copy this both in speech and writing.

Teacher B has used the non-standard form of the verb to sit. Try replacing the verb to see how odd this sounds for *to run* or *to swim*:

> *I want to see you all ran nicely in the hall.*
> *I want to see you all swam nicely in the pool.*

Interestingly, the use of *sat* instead of *sitting* and *stood* instead of *standing* in such constructions can often be heard from television commentators: *I was stood close to where the shots were fired*. This suggests that what is acceptable as Standard English may be changing. A further issue for Teacher B is the use of a slang word 'bums', which many people find offensive. A trainee was recently admonished by a headteacher who told her, 'We don't want the children to use words like "bums". We're better than that. We want to show them a good model of language use'.

Medwell et al. (2011) assert that teachers need to be aware of their children's dialects and the terms which they might use and maintain: 'It is important for teachers to maintain awareness of language usage in society, on television and radio, in newspapers, books and online and to keep in mind the goal of clarity of expression' (Medwell et al., 2011: 10).

Nevertheless, we should consider carefully the challenges some children face when the language they use outside school differs markedly from that used in school. Rosen and Rosen's comment from 1973 still has resonance today:

> The non-standard speaking child is expected to learn more than his standard-speaking peer. He has to translate his own speech into standard then represent it in writing. No wonder he gets behind! (Rosen and Rosen, 1973: 267)

Register

Woolley (2014: 55) suggests that a good starting point for practising oracy skills is to pose questions to children such as '*How do you greet a friend/ teacher?*' or '*Do you speak differently to baby or to your friends?*' In asking such questions, we are encouraging children to think about language variations or what are often termed different *registers*.

Wagner et al. (2010: 17) examined pre-school children's ability to use different linguistic registers and concluded:

> Around age 4 years, children develop an appreciation for register and linguistic style that extends beyond their own social interactions. They understand that individual speakers can flexibly shift their speaking style as a function of their conversational partner; moreover, they understand which specific registers in their native language should be used with different social partners.

Glazzard and Palmer (2015) identify five different registers, which we use depending on whom we are speaking to; what is being discussed; and where and why the conversation is occurring.

Static

This is a formal register associated with particular proceedings such as a religious service, a ceremony or a courtroom. The wording and style are fixed so that people might address each other as *my learned friend* or say a prayer in a specified way.

Formal

This register can also be associated with religious services when the congregation is addressed, and in speeches, sermons and announcements. Typically, this register is used between strangers.

Consultative

Here the conversation can be friendly but formal, such as when you visit a bank manager or doctor. This is also typical of the way teachers speak to students.

Casual

Conversations between friends tend to be casual, with interruptions and interjections. Slang and dialect words might be used and there may be words and phrases and references which outsiders might not understand.

Intimate

This informal register might include verbal and non-verbal communication and tends to be used by close family members.

For young children and for children from different social backgrounds, finding the appropriate register for different situations can be challenging. Manison-Shore (2015) conducted a small-scale study in an affluent and a less affluent area in Bristol and found interesting differences in children's use of language. The more affluent group were able to move between colloquialisms and standard forms swiftly, while children in the less affluent group tended to not to. This accords with Bernstein's (1973) controversial theory of *elaborated* and *restricted* codes, whereby some children are said to be better equipped to switch codes (elaborated) than others (restricted). Another possibility could be that children adjust their language according to social context in order to embed themselves within their community (Maybin, 2007). Manison-Shore (2015: 103) concludes:

> It may be the case that certain resources and choices of activities may favour one social group above another. If so, this has major implications for teachers, raising the question, do children need to be supported to gain access to the vocabulary and the way language is used that is valued in schools?

Ultimately, an inability to use the appropriate register can hinder job prospects and this has been one of the reasons some schools have devised policies to encourage Standard English usage at appropriate times, and to discourage use of local dialect at what are perceived as inappropriate times.

In 2013, a Middlesbrough headteacher, Carol Walker, attracted national attention when she sent letters to parents of children who attended the Sacred Heart Primary School in Teesside, asking them to look out for their children's mispronunciations and slang. She gave examples including 'gizit here' instead of 'give it here' and 'nowt' instead of 'nothing'. Interviewed by the BBC, she said: 'I am not asking children to deny where they come from. I am saying to them there are certain situations where they need to be able to use Standard English.' (BBC News, 2013)

In November 2013, parents at Colley Lane Primary School in Halesowen in the West Midlands were sent a letter which began: *Recently we asked each class teacher to write a list of the top ten most damaging phrases used by children in the classroom. We are introducing a "zero tolerance" in the classroom to get children out of the habit of using the phrases on the list.* The list of banned phrases included:

1. 'They was' instead of 'they were'.
2. 'I cor do that' instead of 'I can't do that'.
3. 'Ya' instead of 'you'.
4. 'Gonna' instead of 'going to'.
5. 'Woz' instead of 'was'.
6. 'I day' instead of 'I didn't'.
7. 'I ain't' instead of 'I haven't'.
8. 'Somefink' instead of 'something'.
9. 'It wor me' instead of 'it wasn't me'.
10. 'Ay?' instead of 'pardon?'

The school emphasised that its aim was to get children to use appropriate language in different situations: 'formal English in the classroom and slang in the school playground'. However, the examples suggest that the school has not made a clear distinction between accent and dialect, and numbers 3 and 5 are examples of a regional accent. It could also be argued that an approach like this could be counterproductive, as children will see it as saying that the language of their family and community is inferior.

There have been other, similar, examples in other areas of the country, arousing debate about the status of regional dialects. However, on the whole, parents appear not to have been offended by such initiatives and those interviewed by the media tended to agree that there were situations where regional dialect was acceptable, but they wanted their children to be able to compete with others when it came to finding jobs and getting places in higher education, and recognised that an ability to use more standard forms was important. So children need to understand that there are different ways of speaking on different occasions and their ability to do so may have implications for the way they are perceived.

Dialects and accents and social acceptability

More prime ministers have been educated at Eton College than at any other school. Eton is among the most expensive schools in Britain and might be expected to adhere strictly to the use of Standard English. However, the school's website provides a *Glossary of Eton Expressions*, guiding new boys on the vocabulary and phrases they will need to understand if they are to be accepted by their fellows. There is even guidance on which terms are used by boys and which by both boys and adults. We learn that a *beak* is a teacher; a *div* is a lesson; *dry bobs* are cricketers; *wet bobs* are rowers; and *slack bobs* neither row nor play cricket.

While most schools may not actually provide a glossary for pupils, the majority of schools and institutions use terms which are understand by those who work there but sometimes not by outsiders. The use of esoteric language creates a sense of identity and belonging and marks people out as being part of a community. Think about part-time jobs you have done and some of the words and phrases which had to be explained to you. In this sense, everyone uses a form of dialect which deviates from Standard English in some circumstances. The key to social acceptance is knowing when to use which form of language or register, and teachers can help children to develop this awareness. As the English National Curriculum for Years 3–4 states:

> At this stage, pupils should start to learn about some of the differences between Standard English and non-Standard English and begin to apply what they have learnt, for example, in writing dialogue for characters. (DfE, 2013: 40)

Drama can be an ideal vehicle for exploring different dialects. By being in role, children are using other people's accents and dialects and may feel more confident about discussing each other's use of language.

Drama: working in different roles

By providing children with scenarios in which they adopt different roles, they can explore the ways in which people speak in a range of situations.

Case study   The town

Fateen wanted her Year 5 class to think about different registers and so made use of a town the children had created as part of a design technology, PSHCE and geography project. The 'town', which was made up of model buildings and streets, with a park, sports ground, shops, schools, etc., was set up on a table in the middle of the classroom. Children produced maps of the town, created bus and train timetables, named streets, shops and schools and then created characters who lived and worked there. As the population grew, children were allowed to 'be' some of the characters and Fateen set up scenarios in which different people would meet. For example, Mr Jones visiting the doctor, Tom Smith meeting his friend Luke Brown, and Mrs Wilson, the head-teacher, taking assembly.

Fateen encouraged children to think about the ways in which they spoke and asked groups to appoint one or two people to listen to conversations and then feed back to participants on the language used. She emphasised that they should not criticise each other, but should simply comment on words and phrases. This led to class and group discussions and eventually to paired and small group writing of dialogue.

Talking about language

Fateen's class were encouraged to talk about language. They discussed some of the words which older characters in the town used. She had been surprised by the way some children could assume the role of, say, a grand-parent and use phrases like 'in my day' and 'when I was a lad', as well as words like wireless and gramophone. She decided to find examples of different registers in television programmes which the children would know and asked friends and colleagues for DVDs which she could use to show excerpts. This led to discussions about accent and dialect as well as register.

Children's literature provides plentiful examples of dialogue which includes different registers, dialects and accents and this can be explored with children as part of literacy lessons. Examples include: Frances Hodgson Burnett's *The Secret Garden* in which there are frequent examples of Yorkshire dialect, which are imitated by Mary; Anthony Browne's *A Walk in the Park* in which the Smiths and the Smythes speak differently; Janet and Allan Ahlberg's *Burglar Bill* which includes such phrases as *all them things* and *that give me a fright* in its dialogue; and, for accent, Sgt Enoch Samways' dropping of aitches and inclusion of them in inappropriate places is hilarious in Roald Dahl's *Danny, the Champion of the World*.

Folk music can also be a good source for exploring dialect. The example of *The Lambton Worm* below can be used as part of music lessons and as a means of looking at dialect and accent. Notice how some words are peculiar to the region of north-east England where the story is set (fash, hoyed, whisht), while others are Standard English words which are misspelled to indicate how they are pronounced with a north-eastern accent (thowt, hyem (home), heuk (hook), doon), and others are corruptions of past tenses (catched for caught).

One Sunday morn young Lambton went
A-fishing' in the Wear;
An' catched a fish upon he's heuk,
He thowt leuk't varry queer.
But whatt'n a kind of fish it was
Young Lambton cuddent tell.
He waddn't fash te carry'd hyem,
So he hoyed it doon a well.
   Whisht! Lads, haad yor gobs,
   An Aa'll tell ye's aall an aaful story
   Whisht! Lads, haad yor gobs,
   An' Aa'll tell ye 'boot the worm.

The complete version with lyrics and sung by a children's choir can be found online (See Stogie in references) and used to help teach the song and tell the story.

Exploring language with children through literature and collecting examples from songs, films and television can be stimulating and thought provoking, and might extend to looking at varieties of Standard English as in the case study below.

Case study   Collecting words and phrases

Ahmed had been reading Judy Blume to his Year 6 class and several examples of US English words had come up and been discussed by the children. Their familiarity with US television programmes meant that they were often able to 'translate' these into UK English, but Ahmed thought it would be helpful for them to develop greater familiarity with US vocabulary, especially as they would meet more US literature in Year 7. He also felt that it would encourage them to make use of dictionaries to look at the origins of words and would give them some insights into the

(Continued)

(Continued)

way in which English has developed from many different languages. This is especially so in the USA where the population grew dramatically though immigration from the 17th century.

Ahmed began by putting up a display with a map and flag of the USA and another of the United Kingdom. He made some vocabulary cards and asked groups of children to sort them and pair them and decide which was used in which place. Children could discuss their own ideas and refer to dictionaries and the internet. Ahmed decided to focus initially on words connected with clothing and food, as he thought these would interest children most and would be likely to appear in the books they read.

US English	UK or British English
pants	trousers
underwear/panties	pants
sweater	pullover/jumper
undershirt	vest
vest	waistcoat
gym shoes	plimsolls, etc.
sneakers	trainers
robe	dressing gown
diaper	nappy
cookie	biscuit
scone	biscuit
zucchini	courgette
candy	sweets
chips	crisps
french fries	chips
jelly	jam
jello	jelly
broil	grill

The children managed the sorting task well and commented that some of the words attributed to US English were already commonly used in the UK, especially those connected with food. Some went on to look at words connected with transport, buildings and school. The class also discussed phrases used in US television and films and noted that some of these had become common in the UK too, especially the insertion of 'like' into many sentences in conversation!

This mini project had several benefits for the children as it:

- helped them to understand vocabulary variations and the language used in US-based films and literature;
- encouraged them to think about words and their meanings;
- helped them appreciate that language is constantly changing;
- gave them an insight into the development of the USA;
- made them think about words which come into English (often called loan words) from other languages.

The British Library website can be a rich source of examples too.

Valuing variety

Our language is constantly changing. Today's slang may be tomorrow's Standard English. The *Oxford English Dictionary (OED)* is regularly updated as new words become commonly used. Its June 2015 additions included more than 300 new words including: *coasteering, crowdfund, e-cigarette, declutter, go-for-it, go-for-broke, carnapping, tea partier* and *webisode* (OED, 2015). English changes continually, with some words entering common usage while others fall out of regular usage. It was interesting to note how some of the words which appeared in the prescribed spelling lists for the first drafts of the current English National Curriculum were dropped from the final version, perhaps because someone pointed out to the authors that words like *haughty* are seldom used in the 21st century.

One of the benefits of teaching a class comprising children from different regions is the scope this gives for exploring language differences and similarities.

Case study   Children and regional dialects

Kate, a Year 3 and 4 teacher in a rural school in the North of England, used the opportunity of a sudden increase in pupil numbers, which resulted from the opening of a new prison in a nearby village, to look at dialects and accents. Around 20 new children from different parts of the

(Continued)

(Continued)

country arrived in the school within a few weeks as their parents took up employment at the prison. Seven of these children came into Kate's class and she was keen that the newcomers settled in quickly and were accepted by existing class members. The children came from the West Midlands (2), Scotland, Newcastle, Manchester, Bristol and London.

Kate, and her class, soon noticed that the new children used different words and phrases when playing games on the playground. Some games had names which the indigenous children didn't recognise and this led to much friendly discussion. At lunchtime, children asked dinner ladies for bread using words like *stottie, bap, barm cake, bread cake* and *cob*. Kate discovered the British Library's website and its dialect maps and facilities for listening to different accents and vocabulary from around the country. She showed these to her class and talked about how people speak differently in different places, but that we all have a common language to use in school. She encouraged children to talk with their parents about the words they used for a range of things and she created a map to display a range of phrases and vocabulary from all parts of the British Isles.

At parents' evening some of the new parents commented that the school project had promoted discussion between colleagues at work, including with prisoners who came from many parts of Britain. This had helped new staff to develop relationships by giving them a topic for conversation.

Kate wanted to encourage children and parents to talk about language and vocabulary, but with less emphasis on regional differences and more on ideolect: the particular individual dialects which we use. She discovered Winchester University's English Project and found a wealth of material to draw upon. She was particularly intrigued by a survey which showed that there were more than 50 different names for the television remote control and that often these were peculiar to different families. Kate asked her class what they called the remote in their house and invited them to talk with their parents and discuss any special names the families gave to particular items. She discovered that very few people actually called the remote control a remote control and used terms such as *clicker, flipper, doodar, switcher, whatsit, wand, dongle* and *hoofer doofer*. It was interesting to discuss how the words might be spelled, since none of them had ever been written down as they were only part of the oral language of the families. This led to some lively discussions and careful thought about appropriate sound-symbol correspondences.

Kate's vocabulary work with her class shows that there are many possibilities for exploring language with children and that parents and carers can become involved too. It is worth considering some of the aspects which could be explored, such as:

- family names for pets and other animals;
- phrases used by families;
- nicknames and names for family members;
- names for household items;
- names for meals and foods;
- names and phrases associated with weather.

Final thoughts...

Ultimately, we need to make ourselves understood and Standard English may be seen as a sort of lingua franca which everyone has access to or understands, even if many never use it consistently. Children need to understand what is regarded as appropriate English when they are writing and in certain social situations.

Emphasising the importance of clarity when communicating is a critical part of the teacher's role. We may not wish to change children's accents or prevent them from using their local dialect when appropriate, but we should be able to discuss the value of clear diction and an appreciation of audience. Accents and dialects are part of the richness of our language, even though their usage can have both positive and negative impacts on people who hear them. As George Bernard Shaw said in his Preface to the play *Pygmalion*: 'It is impossible for an Englishman to open his mouth without making some other Englishman hate or despise him'.

References

BBC News website (2013) Available at: www.itv.com/news/tyne-tees/story/2013-02-06/sacred-heart-primary-middlesbrough-teesside-letter-slang-dialect

Bearne, E. (ed.) (1998) *Use of Language across the Primary Curriculum*. London: Routledge.

Bernstein, B. (1973) *Class, Codes and Control: Volume 1*. St Albans: Paladin.

Brien, J. (2012) *Teaching Primary English*. London: Sage.

British Library www.bl.uk/learning/langlit/sounds/index.html

Browne, A. (2009) *Developing Language and Literacy 3-8* (3rd edn). London: Sage.

Crystal, B. and Crystal, D. (2014) *You Sat Potato: A book about accents*. London: Macmillan.

Crystal, D. (2005) *How Language Works*. London: Penguin.

DfE (2011) Teachers' Standards. www.gov.uk/government/publications/teachers-standards (accessed 13.1.16).

DfE (2013) *The National Curriculum in England Key Stages 1 and 2 Framework Document*. London: DfE.

Dougill, P. and Knott, R. (1988) *The Primary Language Book*. Milton Keynes: Open University Press.

Glazzard, J. and Palmer, J. (2015) *Enriching Primary English*. Northwich: Critical Publishing.

Mallett, M. (2002) *The Primary English Encyclopaedia*. London: David Fulton.

Manison-Shore, L (2015) Talking in class: a study of socio-economic difference in the primary school classroom. *Literacy*. Volume 49, Issue 2: 98–104, April 2015.

Maybin, J. (2007) Towards a sociocultural understanding of children's voice. *Language and Education*, 2 (5): 383–97.

Medwell, J., Moore, G., Wray, D. and Griffiths, V. (2011) *Primary English: Knowledge and Understanding*. Exeter: Learning Matters.

Oxford English Dictionary website (2015) New word list June 2015: public.oed.com/the-oed-today/recent-updates-to-the-oed/june-2015-update/new-words-list-june-2015/#new_words

Rosen, C. and Rosen, H. (1973) *The Language of Primary School Children*. London: Penguin.

Shaw, B. (1916) *Pygmalion*. New York: Brentano (www.bartleby.com/138).

Stogie, D. singing *The Lambton Worm*. YouTube: www.youtube.com/watch?v=BcZcOoP_v2k&app=desktop

Wagner, L., Greene-Havas, M. and Gillespie, R. (2010) Development in children's comprehension of linguistic register. *Child Development,* 2010 Nov–Dec; 81(6):1678–86.

Wells, G. (1982) *Language, learning and education*. Centre for the Study of Language and Communication, University of Bristol.

Woolley, G (2014) *Developing Literacy in the Primary Classroom*. London: Sage.

Further reading

For a fascinating and very readable exploration of accents see:

Crystal, B. and Crystal, D. (2014) *You Sat Potato: a book about accents*. London: Macmillan.

To hear a range of regional dialects and accents from the UK, go to the British Library's website:

www.bl.uk/learning/langlit/sounds/index.html

CHAPTER 9

SPEAKING AND LISTENING: ADDRESSING THE NEEDS OF EAL PUPILS

Kirsty Anderson

Introduction

Sami and Karel play quietly in the construction area of a Year 1 classroom. As they build a tower together they smile encouragingly at each other and point towards the best place for the next wooden brick. From time to time the two children seem to be entering a dialogue, followed by more smiles.

The interaction above is echoed in many primary schools, though not always as quietly! As children get to know each other and co-operate in different groups they test out their language skills, aiming to achieve the primary goals of language use: making meaning and communication. However, Sami and Karel are reliant on gestures, facial expressions and the planned language interventions of their teacher to communicate and be understood. Sami is a bilingual pupil who speaks both Urdu and English, both of which are spoken at home. Sometimes he mixes the two languages when he talks to his English-speaking teachers. His teachers realise he does this if the word in Urdu is a better choice to explain his point – such as when he is talking about family events like Eid celebrations. Karel is a new-to-English pupil, originally from the Czech Republic. His first language is Czech, which is spoken exclusively at home. His main experiences of spoken English language are from school life, which he has been part of for 10 months. Sami and Karel attend a primary school which is experienced in supporting children who have English as an additional language (EAL). The teachers work carefully to plan for the language needs of all pupils at the school, and recognise that making use of opportunities for talk is essential for pupils to communicate and to understand, ultimately to learn.

It is obvious that schools in different areas of the country will have different experiences of working with EAL pupils. So why is this something of which all teachers, in all schools, need to be aware? According to NALDIC (accessed online 2015) one in six pupils, or 1.1 million children and young people in schools today, are EAL learners, speaking upwards of 360 different languages. An increasing number now live in areas where until recently there were few or no such pupils, so all schools have the potential to be multicultural, and teachers should be prepared for the exciting opportunities which can be developed through embracing and exploring the different languages used by children in schools. Since the Swann Report in 1985, schools are expected to ensure EAL learners are included within the classroom, rather than separated from those pupils who have English as their first language. It is vital that children have the opportunity to celebrate diversity, and to understand and accept differences. Exploring the traditions, foods, clothing and languages of other countries offers a richness to children's lives, which is enhanced through sharing experiences of children who have lived in different countries, or have families who live in different countries.

From the example of Sami and Karel above, it seems that children who do not share a common language find a way to communicate with gestures and facial expressions. Children develop their home language or languages (it should be noted that children may speak two or more languages at home) without formal teaching, through use and through continued exposure. Of course, the same can and does happen in the learning of English in school. However, there are several reasons to accelerate this process. Most importantly for teachers, English is the language used both to teach and to assess the progress of pupils. Therefore, for EAL learners to demonstrate their learning they need to be able to communicate in English. Children learn across the curriculum through the medium of English as an additional language and learn English through the medium of the curriculum. Practitioners therefore need to develop the speaking and listening skills of their pupils, and to use their own speaking and listening skills effectively to support the progress of EAL learners, and indeed all pupils. It is important, while children's language skills are developing, that teachers' expectations of their learning across the curriculum are not lowered. In a study published in 2001, Feyisa Demie identified that some ethnic minority groups actually outperform native English speakers. However, according to Demie (2001), the more fluent children are, the better their achievements. Cummins (2000) suggests that it takes two years for an EAL pupil to be conversationally fluent in English, but on average five to seven years to achieve what Cummins describes as *cognitive and academic language proficiency (CALP)*. Yet, after two years, schools are expected to enter EAL learners in standardised assessments.

Demie's (2013) empirical data suggests there is a significant difference in speed of acquisition of fluent English between pupils based on the language they speak.

> The largest groups in the LA [local authority], Turkish, Lingala, Spanish, Bengali and Portuguese speakers, take a longer time, between six and eight years, compared with French, Yoruba, Somali, Akan and Polish speakers, who may acquire a proficient level of fluency in English in between five and six years. These data further confirm that EAL pupils from African Commonwealth countries achieve full fluency in English earlier than those from many other countries. (Demie, 2013: 66)

Differences in speaking and listening attainment on entry into primary school aged four or five are inevitable and are influenced by multiple and various factors for all children. The factors affecting spoken English can include whether a child has siblings, attendance at playgroups or nurseries and interactions with parents. It is important to understand that EAL learners will also have this range of different factors affecting their language skills and, alongside this, EAL learners have different language needs.

Moreover, even in their home language – which is sometimes called the 'mother tongue', 'first language' or 'home language' – each EAL pupil's knowledge and experience will be different. Ofsted (2014) noted that EAL pupils are not a homogeneous group. Statistics from NALDIC (2015) indicate that upwards of 360 different languages are spoken by the 1.1 million children who are EAL learners. In some cases they will speak exclusively in the family's first language at home, while others will have families who speak English alongside their first language and some will speak two or more languages. It is important that teachers are aware of their pupils' language backgrounds.

Recognising children's different strengths and needs is an essential aspect of a primary teacher's role. Standard 5 of The Teachers' Standards (2013: 12) states that teachers must *adapt teaching to respond to the strengths and needs of all pupils* including showing *understanding of the distinctive needs of pupils with English as an Additional Language (EAL)*. This chapter explains the distinctive needs of EAL pupils in speaking and listening; considers the difference between language and learning needs; explores challenges which may be part of the day-to-day life of a primary school teacher in an increasingly diverse population; aims to explore the benefits for teachers and children alike of celebrating diverse classrooms; and offers guidance on effective teaching approaches.

What is meant by EAL pupils?

As Ofsted (2014) notes, EAL pupils are not one single group. Conteh (2015) lists different terms which have been used to describe different groups of EAL learners, including new arrivals, isolated learners in schools with very few EAL learners, and children whose families have lived in this country for two or three generations. It is essential to ensure that teachers recognise the different needs of different EAL pupils, and avoid making assumptions that might lead to all EAL pupils being grouped together.

It is possible to broadly categorise EAL pupils into the following groups, which will be considered in more detail in later sections of the chapter:

- Pupils who are new to English.
- Pupils becoming familiar with English.
- Pupils becoming confident as users of English.
- Advanced bilingual pupils - experienced and near fluent users of English. (Adapted from Hester, 1990)

In order to plan and teach effectively for the individual needs of EAL pupils, the importance of understanding pupils' prior knowledge and experience cannot be underestimated.

Understanding children's experience

Primary school teachers need to understand the complexity of children's knowledge and experience, and not simply in relation to language. Questions to ask include: *Has the child attended school before? What language or languages does the child and the family speak? How well developed is their knowledge of their home language? Does the home language have a written form? Is the child literate in any language?* Establishing this baseline of background knowledge can help teachers to understand the difference between a language need and a learning need. This is not only about recognising a pupil's attainment in English, but also recognising and developing the home language. EAL learners may have limited English skills, but might be proficient in reading, writing, speaking and listening in the home language. It is also important to appreciate that some EAL learners have had experience of school before becoming part of your classroom. These experiences are likely to be diverse. For instance, in the Czech Republic formal schooling does not begin until age 7, while in Saudi Arabia schooling begins much earlier, but is very different from the play-based learning which is common in the Early Years. Cultural differences are not always extreme; however, they will inevitably impact on the readiness of EAL learners to speak and to listen in the classroom. Where the child has arrived from another country or has family in another country or countries, it can also be helpful to find out about that country. Teachers can help new pupils to feel welcome and valued through the use of maps, pictures and artefacts from other countries, which enable all children to understand the wider world.

New to English pupils and the 'silent period'

Starting school can be an exciting and challenging time for any child. Understandably, children and their families are anxious about finding friends, managing routines and being in unfamiliar environments. For an EAL learner who is new to English, this anxiety can be magnified because of various factors: new to English pupils will have little or no experience in a school in the UK and may be new to the country, and might have moved for a range of complex and challenging reasons. Even when the move has been carefully planned and children come from a country with a similar education system, the language challenge they face is considerable. In oral language the difficulties include breaking the flow of language up into words and understanding them. Oral language often moves quickly, making it difficult to follow and difficult to join in. Unlike reading, children cannot go at their own pace and return to unclear parts to study them more carefully. In addition, oral language is often less formal than written language, with fragmented sentences and colloquial language making comprehension more challenging. On the other hand, oral language is often simpler and more repetitive than written language, and is supported by intonation, facial expressions and gesture.

In this transition period it is crucial to provide formal and informal opportunities to develop English speaking and listening skills for new to English pupils. It is most likely that they will begin their spoken language journey with 'survival language'. Sometimes called 'playground language', these are the words and phrases useful for navigating school life, and importantly for making friends. Strategies to support children through this initial phase include:

- making sure the child knows your name;
- demonstrating the meaning of simple instructions such as 'sit down';
- matching the child up with a buddy for playtimes, classroom routines and so on;
- providing a good language model, as discussed in Chapter 1 – for example, speaking at a moderate pace, articulating clearly, and repeating things carefully when necessary;

- identifying and modelling key vocabulary and language structures of texts or activities;
- using visual prompts such as pictures, objects, diagrams and graphic organisers;
- integrating the child into class activities as far as possible;
- giving any additional support (e.g. from a teaching assistant) within the class rather than by withdrawing the child;
- grouping the child with others who provide good models of language and learning.

According to NALDIC (2014), children who are new to English are likely to experience what can be called a 'silent period'. This may last for up to a year. EAL learners transitioning through this phase will be listening and formulating their understanding of the language they hear and begin to understand, but might not communicate in 'academic' English (the classroom language used by their peers). Although the pupils may seem to be passive, Mills and Mills (1993) point out that pupils are likely to be carefully observing the routines and behaviours of others, which can lead to copying and repeating language used by their classmates – one of the first stages of development.

Teachers should expect this phase and support children sensitively through it, not pressurising them to speak or over-reacting when they do. As children begin to speak in the classroom context, many of the strategies outlined in Chapter 1 for supporting early language development are relevant. Returning to the example at the beginning of the chapter, when Karel builds a tower in the construction area and exclaims 'brick top' as it is finished, a teacher might expand this by saying, 'Yes, you put a brick on the top!'

What can teachers do?

Case study   Planning for Karel

Karel joined his Year 1 class at the start of the school year. Originally from the Czech Republic, Karel has moved to England with his family. His parents speak Czech at home and have little experience of English language. Karel has no experience of formal schooling.

Karel's teacher, Lee, is experienced with EAL learners. He and his colleagues plan for language needs alongside learning needs in every curriculum area. Each week Lee maps out the different classroom activities on offer to the pupils and records the language which might need to be taught. Verbal interaction is encouraged and Lee works with his TA to model language for the pupils. Karel observes Lee talking to Sami, an advanced bilingual pupil in the construction area. Karel joins Sami in the construction area. Lee skilfully enables Karel to join the conversation by inviting Karel to put bricks onto the tower Sami is constructing. Karel is able to follow Lee's instruction to pick up bricks. Lee encourages Sami to use adjectives and comparatives to describe the tower. As Lee and Sami talk, Lee uses actions to describe the build. Every time another brick is added, Lee raises his hands, describing it as 'higher', 'bigger' and a 'skyscraper'. Rather than including only one of the children, Lee carefully ensures that Karel is part of the social interaction as he extends Sami's well-developed vocabulary. Although Karel uses Czech in this conversation he makes use of body language and facial expressions to indicate where Lee should place the bricks as the tower grows too tall for him to reach.

Lee highlights the language which Karel has listened to and the words he has copied (like brick, high and top). He plans other small-group activities that Karel can join so that he will have the opportunity to make use of his developing vocabulary and to become more confident, as shown below:

Year group	Curriculum area	Activity	Function of language which might be used	Structure of language	Vocabulary
1	Structured play/DT	Building towers	Planning, giving instructions, giving opinions	I think it could... Let's try... Put this...	Bricks, high, higher, tower, strong, fall
1	PE	Gymnastics: make the biggest shapes...	Planning, giving instructions, giving opinions	I think we could... Let's try... Put your feet....	High, higher, big, bigger, strong, stronger

The case study above demonstrates the value of play in supporting language acquisition. This is a key feature of early years education and Mistry and Sood (2012: 291) argue that 'some effective practices in the Early Years need to be embedded in the whole primary sector, which would ensure that pupils who have EAL continue to make progress'. They maintain that school leaders need to *ensure that at the heart of the learning process is how pupils learn and develop, which appears to be a key feature of the Early Years culture* (Mistry and Sood, 2012: 291).

Becoming familiar with the English language

In this stage, pupils may be enthusiastically trying to communicate, even though their language skills are still limited. They may mix English with their first language in an attempt to maintain fluency. The desire and necessity to communicate needs to be welcomed and supported so that even when making errors, mixing languages or relying on gestures, pupils have the chance to convey their messages in a safe environment. Correcting children's language suggests that we are more interested in their mistakes than in what they are trying to say, and can inhibit children's attempts to speak (Primary National Strategy, 2007). Teaching strategies to support children in this stage will include activating prior knowledge at the beginning of a lesson, to introduce key vocabulary and provide a meaningful context for the talk; providing shared experiences so that talk before, during and after the experience is carefully linked to what the children have seen and done; and scaffolding language with talk frames, which parallel writing frames in providing structures for different types of talk, and prompts which provide models of appropriate language. The following are examples of talk frames:

Describing something	Reporting back	Giving an opinion
What is it?	What I/we did	The question is...
What does it look like?	How I/we did it	My view is...
Where do you find it?	Any difficulties I/we had	I think this because...
What is it used for?	What worked well	(give as many reasons as possible)
	What I/we learned	

Confident English users

EAL learners who have what Cummins (2000) described as basic interpersonal communication skills (BICS) are confident in the everyday English needed for social interaction, and are likely to contribute to group discussions, give reasons for their thoughts and make use of their developing vocabularies. At this stage, they are likely to listen and follow instructions as easily as their peers who have English as their first language. However, it is important to ensure that the EAL learners working at this stage are still supported in developing the cognitive and academic language proficiency referred to earlier. Careful assessment of the language demands of different tasks, and the vocabulary and language structures associated with them, and modelling of appropriate language, continue to be essential through this stage.

In the case study below, a teacher has identified a specific aspect of language for development. She considers the pairing of pupils carefully, and selects a task which gives ample opportunity for practice.

Case study   Paired barrier games

Alice is in her second year of teaching in a Year 4 class. The school has a diverse population and approximately 60 per cent of pupils are EAL. The pupils in Alice's class have a wide range of abilities. To maximise opportunities for talk, Alice plans paired barrier games. (Barrier games involve children sitting opposite each other with screens between. One child then gives instructions to the other. Each child has the same set of materials in front of them. The children then take turns giving the other players very specific directions on how to arrange the materials in front of them.) Roxana and Erika work as a pair. Roxana, originally from Romania, has been in school for two years, and although she is quiet Alice is certain that Roxana's English is developing well. Even when uncertain of the correct English, she substitutes other English words rather than mixing her first and second languages. Erika, from Slovakia, has also attended the school for two years. Erika has a smaller vocabulary than Roxana, but is confident in her use of English.

Alice gives clear instructions as part of the barrier game, which is intended to develop understanding of prepositions. Each pair has a matching story character and map. Without looking (using a barrier) they have to take it in turns to give directions for the character to move around the story map. To differentiate this task, Alice uses more detailed maps for those with more sophisticated English language skills. For the pupils in her class who are new to English, Alice still uses barrier games, but records simple directions on sound button recording devices for the pairs to follow.

Activities of this nature have a clear language focus, but are set in an enjoyable and purposeful context, which motivates and challenges pupils. Visual resources support understanding, and the task provides good opportunity to practise the target language repeatedly. Prepositions can be difficult for pupils whose home language does not use them, or uses them in a different position in the sentence as in South Asian languages. Other grammatical features which can be particularly challenging for EAL learners include verbs, where the most common verbs (*to be, to have, to go, to get*) are irregular and other verbs have irregular past tenses (*wrote, kept, sang*). Modal verbs (*may, might, can, could, will, would, shall, should, must, ought to*) can pose particular problems in negative statements and in questions. Determiners are also difficult to use accurately – *the North Sea* but not *the Yorkshire*, for example – and the order of words in a noun phrase is also hard to grasp (*the big red car* not *the red big car*).

Advanced bilingual learners

The group referred to as advanced bilingual or multilingual learners includes children for whom English is their first and most dominant language rather than an additional language – for example, children whose families have been settled in this country for generations but who have strong links with their countries of origin. Multilingual learners can move freely between the languages they know depending on their audience and the purpose of their talk. Their languages can be a positive resource for learning in the classroom (Conteh, 2015: 58). However, languages often include terms that can prevent free movement between languages. In the case study below, a teacher finds that some of the words and phrases which might be familiar to native English speakers can prove challenging for EAL learners.

Case study   Extending Ahmed's language

Ahmed is currently in Year 5 at an inner-city primary school. He started the school in nursery and has made very good progress throughout his time there. His family are originally from the Sylheti region of Bangladesh, though Ahmed was born in the UK. He has visited Bangladesh twice. At home his family speaks a mixture of English and Sylheti.

Ahmed's teacher, Maryann, plans to teach her class debating skills. She uses a recent event as the topic – the closure of the local swimming pool. Maryann recognises that the class need to learn the conventions of debate, including the use of emotive language in order to persuade the audience to agree with their points of view. Maryann acts as a role model initially, outlining what she might say to the council leaders about the proposed pool closure. She uses phrases including 'give a dog a bad name' to explain how others might react to a decision to close the pool and 'shoot yourself in the foot' when trying to outline the need for a local swimming pool. Maryann asks her class to identify the most powerful phrases she has used. Ahmed rightly identifies 'give a dog a bad name'. However, when Maryann pushes for a definition Ahmed explains that it means dogs are not nice so it is comparing the council leaders to dogs. Maryann explains the real meaning: that if you say bad things about someone they will stick, and why she used it – to convey the feeling that the public might start to believe negative views about the council. Before continuing with the debate, Maryann decides she needs to develop the pupils' understanding of idioms to enhance the impact of their spoken language skills.

Maryann shares a range of idioms with the class such as 'put your best foot forward', 'moving the goalposts' and 'mum's the word'. She first asks the class to act out each idiom. Next she tasks the groups with finding out what the idioms mean. As there are a range of EAL learners in the class, Maryann asks those who are developing their confidence in English to go and find out from other adults, and by researching using the internet, what the idioms mean in order to improve their speaking and listening skills. In order to develop Ahmed's understanding, she asks his group to try to find the origin of each idiom. Maryann is interested in Ahmed's original answer about dogs and asks him to investigate if there are any equivalent idioms in Sylheti which he can share with his classmates. As an experienced teacher of EAL pupils, Maryann recognises the value of understanding and celebrating a pupil's home language and cultural experiences.

Flynn (2007) notes some of the issues surrounding the words and phrases which are familiar to native speakers but which might prove confusing for those acquiring English as an additional language. She asserts that: *A surface confidence with spoken English may disguise a lack of knowledge about technical and idiomatic English that will hinder development in reading comprehension* (Flynn, 2007: 179).

Such barriers to understanding are not peculiar to English and are often encountered by English speakers when holidaying abroad, even when they feel confident in their use of the native language. For example, in French even fluent foreigners might be confused by:

- *donner sa langue au chat* (give your tongue to the cat) – to give up;
- *avoir les dents longues* (to have long teeth) – to be ambitious;
- *être soupe au lait* (to be milky soup) – to be quick-tempered.

It is important, therefore, that we are mindful of potential misunderstandings when we use phrases which, while familiar to English first language users, may be confusing for EAL learners. We clearly need 'to pull our socks up' in this area!

The place of home languages in children's learning

It is important that families understand that bilingualism is an asset to the child, and that the home or first language has an important role in the child's language. Some families may be reluctant to give schools a picture of the child's language background, and teachers need to show an interest in those other languages and make it clear that the school is proud that its pupils speak other languages as well as English. Families may be keen that children learn English as quickly as possible, and feel that supporting the home language will delay the acquisition of English. They may even consider that it would be helpful to use English in the home, and teachers need to understand that using their strongest language in order for children to engage in rich communication within the family is the best way to support children's learning. Equally, if there are opportunities for children to use their first language in school this will support learning, including learning of English. Bilingual staff can be a significant asset, and their deployment needs to be carefully considered. For example, it may be more helpful to provide pre-teaching and preparation for a class lesson rather than language support within the lesson, so the EAL learner can be more fully engaged in that lesson. It is also important to be sensitive to concerns when some languages are supported by bilingual staff and others are not.

Guidance on assessing EAL learners

In 2000 QCA published *A Language in Common: Assessing English as an Additional Language*. This guidance included the Extended Scales, which offer classroom practitioners a useful structure against which to assess the EAL pupils they are teaching. The Extended Scales were designed to lead towards National Curriculum levels. The Extended Scales remain a valuable source of reference against which to assess the needs of EAL pupils who are new to or have little experience in the English language. The document is available to download from: www.naldic.org.uk

Final thoughts...

Speaking and listening skills are vital to the success of every pupil in primary school. Teachers need to plan opportunities to ensure children can develop these skills and therefore become better skilled at communicating and understanding what they learn. All children are different and will need careful support to develop the skills they already have. To make the most of the rich resource of the pupils themselves teachers can plan opportunities to learn new languages, celebrate cultural diversity and importantly to practise the use of the English language. This is just as important for children whose first language is English as it is for EAL pupils. Creating a talking classroom will inevitably benefit all pupils, and there will be ample opportunities to demonstrate and develop essential language skills, useful in all areas of life.

References

Conteh, J. (2015) *The EAL Teaching Book: promoting success for multilingual learners in primary and secondary schools*. London: Sage.

Cummins, J. (2000) *Language, Power and Pedagogy: Bilingual children in the crossfire*. Clevedon, England: Multilingual Matters.

Demie, F. (2001) Ethnic and gender differences in educational achievement and implications for school improvement strategies. *Educational Research*, 43(1) 91–106.

Demie, F. (2013) English as an additional language pupils: how long does it take to acquire English fluency? *Language and Education*, 22(1): 59–69, DOI: 10.1080/09500782.2012.682580

DfE (2013) *Teachers' Standards*. First published July 2011, introduction updated 2013. Available online at: https://www.gov.uk/government/uploads/system/uploads/attachment_data/file/301107/Teachers__Standards.pdf

Flynn, N. (2007) Good practice for pupils learning English as an additional language: Lessons from effective literacy teachers in inner-city primary schools. *Journal of Early Childhood Literacy*, 2007 (7): 177. DOI: 10.1177/1468798407079286

Hester, H. (1990) *Patterns of Learning*. London: CLPE.

Mills, R.W. and Mills, J. (1993) *Bilingualism in the Primary School*. London: Routledge.

Mistry, M. and Sood, K. (2012) Raising standards for pupils who have English as an Additional Language (EAL) through monitoring and evaluation of provision in primary schools. *Education 3–13: International Journal of Primary, Elementary and Early Years Education*, 40 (3): 281–93, DOI: 10.1080/03004279.2010.523434

NALDIC: www.naldic.org.uk/research-and-information/eal-statistics/ (accessed October 2015).

Ofsted (2014) *English as an Additional Language: Briefing for Section 5 Inspection*. Available online at: http://www.naldic.org.uk/eal-teaching-and-learning/outline-guidance/eal-ofsted/ (accessed 13.1.16).

Primary National Strategy (2007) *Supporting Children Learning English as an Additional Language: Guidance for practitioners in the Early Years Foundation Stage*. London: DCSF.

QCA (2000) *A Language in Common: assessing English as an Additional Language*. Available online at: http://webarchive.nationalarchives.gov.uk/20100202100434/qcda.gov.uk/5739.aspx

Report of the Committee of Enquiry into the Education of Children from Ethnic Minority Groups (1985) *The Swann Report: Education for All*. Available online at: http://www.educationengland.org.uk/documents/swann/swann1985.html

CHAPTER 10

DIGITAL COMMUNICATION

John Bennett

Communication is an aspect of life that is in constant change. The fundamental communication forms of language, using reading, writing, speaking and listening, remain constant for the majority, but the media through which we communicate in those areas change and adapt. The latest phase in this evolution is characterised by the application of digital technology. On-screen reading, word-processing and mass communication through the internet and global mobile phone network are all key parts of modern society. Printed texts, handwriting and face-to-face communication all, of course, still have their place, but the move to digital media for all of these forms has been revolutionary. Education has not always managed to keep up with this rapid change and it is a challenge for teachers to ensure that both what they teach and how they teach takes account of the changes in forms of communication which are already a part of children's lives, and will certainly continue to develop in the future.

This chapter will explore the opportunities in teaching language-based communication skills (rather than visual communication, which of course also occurs digitally) in relation to the use of technology, both as a tool to enhance that teaching and as a necessary feature of any modern education in communication. It will focus more on the spoken word than on reading and writing, as the development of speaking and listening skills allied with technology is not often as well explored as technology-focused and enhanced development of reading and writing.

Communication, education and technology

For some time, the English National Curriculum included Information and Communication Technology (ICT) as a subject in itself (DfEE/QCA, 1999). The emphasis of the communication aspect of that tended to relate to on-screen reading and writing, rather than oral communication. This was probably partly due to successive pushes for improvement in reading and writing, more than speaking and listening, but was, to a large extent, due to the fact that the hardware and software required for the successful use of technology to support oracy was more limited, complicated or expensive. With the growth in multimedia elements through CD-ROMs and then on web pages, listening was certainly a skill which could be practised through the use of technology, and schools have, for a long time, made use of talking books via various media formats. Some schools made good use of cassette recorders and video cameras to record children and in some cases to work with children on editing and refining spoken language, but modern digital technology makes such activities much more accessible.

ICT no longer exists as a National Curriculum subject, but the latest version of the National Curriculum, within its aims for the computing section, clearly states that children should be *responsible, competent, confident and creative users of information and communication technology* (DfE, 2013: 178). This acknowledges that technology is not just a means of dealing with information, but also of communicating. Unfortunately, the National Curriculum does not expand on this key aspect of modern life and the important need for the development of skills in communicating using technology. Teachers must not take this lack of emphasis as meaning that information and communication technology is no longer as important as it was, with computing superseding it. In fact, a good way to think of this is as digital technology providing the medium and tools for the curriculum, in the same way as pen and paper had traditionally done. We would not expect to see detail about media and tools in the curriculum content. The programmes of study in the National Curriculum only use generic statements about creating digital content, rather than specifically identifying text creation and manipulation skills.

The SAMR model (Puentedura, 2013) presents a way of considering different levels of the operation of technology in increasing order of change: *substitution, augmentation, modification* and *redefinition*. Each of these levels has its place, but the more devices, apps and programs become available, the more we move from simply using technology as a substitute (e.g. word processing and printing, instead of paper and pen, video conferencing instead of face-to-face meetings), to *redefinition* (new activities, such as the collaborative creation of an instructional video). Many of the activities described in earlier chapters of this book could be undertaken with the addition of technology, but that should never happen just for the sake of it. A way of thinking about whether technology would be appropriate to use for a given activity would be to consider the following questions. If the answer to any of the questions is *yes*, then there is reason to consider using technology to enhance or extend the activity.

- Will using the technology enhance the experience in some way?
- Will using the technology increase children's engagement?
- Will using the technology help the children learn or develop skills in using technology, while not interfering with the development of communication skills?
- Will using the technology enhance children's understanding of how technology supports communication in society?

Beyond this, teachers also need to be mindful of the way technology can lead to new activities, which can enhance the learning process, such as *synchronous collaborative writing* and *video conferencing* or *collaborative writing*, where children work together on one piece of text, but using individual devices – editing and commenting on each other's contributions.

Children and communication through technology

Digital communication takes many forms, most of which are probably within your own experience, such as:

- websites;
- text messages;
- emails;
- video conferencing;
- video calls (Skype and FaceTime, perhaps);
- webinars;
- sending video or picture messages;
- social networking;
- online social activities (such as online gaming);
- blogging or microblogging (Twitter);
- podcasts;
- video streaming/downloading.

In all of these instances the digital form is being used for one- or two-way communication. All of these experiences are available and increasingly being used as part of the communication landscape of children. The world children experience outside school and the world of their future requires children to develop skills in their use, explore the potential for expanding their communication methods and also be aware of the benefits and dangers that digital communication presents.

EU Kids Online – Zero to Eight

EU Kids Online's 2013 report showed the findings of a study of the youngest children's engagement with the online world. It noted that

> there has been a substantial increase in internet usage by children under nine years old. This increase is not uniform across countries but seems to follow usage patterns among older age cohorts – in countries where more children overall use the internet, they also go online younger' (Holloway et al., 2013: 4).

Research in the UK does indicate a growth in internet use by older children (Ofcom, 2014), so it is reasonable to assume that more primary age children in the UK are accessing the internet.

The EU Kids Online report also showed that the younger children were engaged in a wide variety of online activities, including: *watching videos, playing games, searching for information, doing their homework and socialising within children's virtual worlds. The range of activities increases with age* (Holloway et al., 2013: 4).

While a significant amount of the report is rightly concerned with the safety aspects of young children being online, it also explores the benefits and notes that further research is needed in that area.

It is important, of course, to consider e-safety, in the use of the web in particular. In a recent survey, one in ten 8–11-year-olds reported seeing something inappropriate or worrying online (Ofcom, 2014), but that same survey showed that children are becoming more aware of the potential dangers of being online and part of the communication networks provided through social media. There is no space in this chapter for a full consideration of the issues around e-safety, but with appropriate permissions and safeguards, alongside good training for children, teachers can mitigate those dangers and ensure that positive and safe communication using digital technology is possible. While there are negative aspects to the use of technology by children for communication purposes (DCSF, 2008), children today are growing up in a world where previous norms are changing rapidly and it would be remiss of educators not to take the fullest possible account of the changing nature of communication by providing suitable learning activities which are designed after due consideration has been given to the risks and appropriate actions have been taken to minimise those risks.

Children's interaction with technology (Ofcom)

A 2014 survey, 'Children and Parents: Media Use and Attitudes Report', investigated how 5–15-year-olds interact with media, including digital technology for communication (Ofcom, 2014). Comparing results from previous years, it showed a growing trend in children's ownership of tablet computers, use of the internet and a preference for using mobile phones for social and creative activities (above other forms of technology). Over 40 per cent of Year 6 children owned a smartphone. About one-fifth of Key Stage 1 children and about one-third of Key Stage 2 children owned tablets. Although the results varied by age and the most significant uses were with children older than primary age, there was still a clear picture from this research of the growing use and impact of digital forms of communication with children.

In the survey, one-fifth of 8–11-year-olds said they had a social media profile, which is, of course, a key form of communication for many adults. Facebook was most often cited as the platform used.

Ofcom use the phrase *media literacy*, defining this is as *the ability to use, understand and create media and communications in a variety of contexts* (Ofcom, 2014: 20). In effect, this chapter is promoting the development of media literacy in primary education, to meet the communication needs of the children and society. It is important to note that much digital communication, such as text messages and tweets, often has more in common with oral communication than with non-digital reading and writing, in that it is brief, instantaneous and informal, replicating the to and fro of conversation. For that reason this chapter considers reading and writing as well as speaking and listening.

Digital communication

Reading

The growth in digital communication has led to the development of new media to read from and also new ways of reading. Adults and children now access reading material in a wide variety of digital formats (text messages, tweets, emails, status updates, web pages, etc.), as well as replacements for books, comics, magazines and newspapers in the form of eReaders, such as the Kindle. Although images and increasingly video and sound also communicate information digitally through many of these formats, the digitised word is still used throughout.

For teachers, a key response to the growth in digital texts and the importance of those in the children's future must be to use digital texts as a part of the range of texts the children interact with in schools. A second key response must be to teach children how to use digital texts in the most productive ways. This must include developing children's understanding of how digital texts differ from analogue formats and the opportunities these differences offer. In many cases, the digital equivalent, or digitally enhanced version of a particular activity, can appropriately be taught alongside the analogue skills; for example, looking at dictionaries and spellcheckers together. This approach helps the children develop an understanding of when it is and when it isn't appropriate to use technology.

Children increasingly have access to digital reading materials in schools. Reading digital texts now starts from a very early age and continues throughout primary school for most children in the UK, at least through the use of interactive whiteboards in most primary classrooms. These devices, when used to their maximum effect, can enhance children's understanding and help them develop skills in digital reading, which they can then apply in their individual work. For example, a teacher can model navigating a web page, by talking through the skimming and scanning that is done to identify key points or hyperlinks and also point out the potentially valueless hyperlinks (or *clickbait*, as things which draw the eye and make you want to click on them are now termed). Schools are investing more and more in mobile devices, which offer children independent opportunities to engage with the digital world, and much of that will include reading. Many reading schemes, such as Rising Stars (www.risingstars-uk.com/) and Oxford Reading Tree (www.oxfordowl.co.uk/), offer eBooks or eBook versions of many of their texts, which children can access anywhere. In some cases, such as Bug Club (Pearson Education), online support materials also provide for assessment of reading comprehension, which teachers can access online.

Digital reading includes different and enhanced approaches to communication through on-screen text, which children need to learn about. Examples of aspects of digital reading which should have a place within learning and teaching in primary classrooms include developing children's:

- experience of multimedia and interactive texts;
- understanding that many digitals texts, such as web pages, can be read in a non-linear way;
- understanding of the range of tools that support the reading process, including look-up tools, such as links to dictionaries and encyclopaedia;
- understanding of the range of text marking tools, such as bookmarks, adding comments and sharing, afforded by word processing and desktop publishing programs;
- skills in searching, skimming and scanning, to find relevant information quickly, in ways which use the navigation features such as hyperlinks and 'find' or 'search' functions;
- skills in reading web pages, navigating non-linear texts online, identifying relevant information and discerning bias, recognising advertising.

Teachers should look for opportunities to introduce, explore and build on children's skills, knowledge and understanding of the above and any other emerging developments in digital reading, to ensure that children can engage with modern approaches to communication through reading in the most effective ways.

Writing

Digital writing plays a major role in communication and the process of creating text using digital means must be an integral part of any school's curriculum, helping children to develop the skills, knowledge and under-standing which they will apply through their own digitally created writing as children and, almost certainly, as a significant feature of their adult life.

Writing digitally, as with other forms of digital communication, continues to evolve. One of the first readily available forms of computer program was the word-processor and since its introduction the ways of creating text on-screen have grown. There are few jobs which do not require a person to type at some point, and much of the personal communication people send to each other is now word-processed. More recently, social networking sites, whether they are microblogging ones such as Twitter or more per-sonal web spaces such as Facebook, are increasingly being accessed and used by adults and children. Although the largest of these, Facebook, has age restrictions, which should not allow children's use, even in 2013 a sur-vey found that almost one in three 7–11-year-olds claimed to have their own Facebook profile and that number is likely to have grown (Broadbent et al., 2013). These are new forms of mass communication and much of the user-created content is in text form.

In schools, almost any writing activity can be approached using technol-ogy, but as noted earlier in this chapter, the appropriateness of using the technology needs careful consideration. This is particularly true for writing, where underdeveloped keyboard skills can slow down the process of com-position. In order for children to gain the skills required for digital writing, there are many areas of experience schools should ensure are offered as part of the curriculum. Examples of aspects of digital writing which should have a place within learning and teaching in primary classrooms include developing children's:

- keyboard skills;
- understanding of the range of text manipulation tools afforded by word-processing and desktop publishing programs;
- understanding how different fonts and font enhancements (bold, italic, colour, etc.) can have an impact on the reader's experience with the text;

- understanding of the many functions of a word processor which can assist in the editing process, particular features such as select, find (and replace), copy and paste;
- knowledge of the potential wider audience for their written work, particularly when published online;
- skills in collaborative writing, as afforded through Web 2.0 tools such as the word processor in Google Docs;
- experience of creating digital texts, which are not just digital versions of analogue counterparts (such as word-processing poems and stories), but are forms of text which are usually digitally presented, including: text messages, emails, blog entries, web pages, enhanced digital presentations (e.g. using Prezi – www.prezi.com) and interactive books.

A 'new' addition to the way in which people communicate, for many on a daily basis, is the use of *emojis* or *emoticons*. These visual devices add meaning to short pieces of text and can even be used to replace text completely at times. It will be interesting to see how these develop over time, as they have already moved from only appearing in text messages, to now appearing in emails and also popping up in advertising. Alongside emoticons, abbreviations are also heavily used by some people in text messages and other short forms of text used online, such as in online gaming chat windows and in tweets – *lol, rofl, brb*, etc. OMG has even become a 'word' used in some people's conversations. Research (Plester et al., 2009) has shown these 'textisms' not to have the negative effect on literacy which might have been expected. It is therefore no surprise that textspeak and emoticons have started to appear in scheme reading books, such as the 'Rigby Navigator' series from Pearson, to help develop comprehension of these forms of communication. Language evolves and the range of aspects of communication considered in primary schools needs to keep up with this.

A fascinating possibility for the future of writing is the development of speech to text. For some time, reluctant or less able writers have been able to use programs such as *Clicker* (www.cricksoft.com) to input text without the need to write or type every word or phrase, helping support a more fluent approach to writing for those children and building confidence in the ability to compose, if not the physical act of transcription. With speech to text programs or apps available on most platforms and providing good quality translations of spoken to written word, children have ready access to this approach to composition. Given that poor handwriting can inhibit motivation to write (Medwell and Wray, 2008), while it is still important to ensure children develop physical writing skills, using speech to text is one way to promote success in composition.

As with reading, teachers should look for opportunities to introduce, explore and build on children's skills, knowledge and understanding of aspects of digital text creation, being aware of developments in both the contexts for text creation and the methods and skills required to be effective digital writers.

Speaking and listening

The contexts for both speaking and listening have seen significant changes and the ways in which adults communicate have gone through a revolution due to the increasing power and reducing cost of communications technology. The growth in mobile phone use is a prime example. Video communication software, such as Skype and FaceTime, makes real-time conversations across the globe both affordable and technically very simple in general use, and these are things which many children will have experience of outside school. The use of digital technology to support oral communication is therefore an essential aspect of education in modern primary schools.

The English National Curriculum (DfE, 2013: 10) states that:

> Pupils should be taught to speak clearly and convey ideas confidently using Standard English. They should learn to justify ideas with reasons; ask questions to check understanding; develop vocabulary and build knowledge; negotiate; evaluate and build on the ideas of others; and select the appropriate register for effective communication. They should be taught to give well-structured descriptions and explanations and develop their understanding through speculating, hypothesising and exploring ideas. This will enable them to clarify their thinking as well as organise their ideas for writing.

Every aspect of these expectations regarding developing speaking and listening can be supported or enhanced through the application of digital technology. The following sections explore some examples of how this can happen in practice.

Digital recording

Selecting 'the appropriate register' is one expectation which can be very well supported through the use of digital devices. The register can simply mean the style of language used, for example formal or informal, but this must be seen as going further, to include the stylistic devices used within speech. Children are expected to develop skills in expression, in order to help 'convey ideas confidently', yet unlike writing, apart from through repetition and change, there is no supportive way to edit what has been said. This is where simple modern technology can really enhance the learning, through the use of digital recording in a variety of forms.

One of the educational advantages of children recording their speech is the fact that they can immediately listen back, decide what can be improved and then re-record it. Effectively, this mirrors the drafting process in writing. This is oral drafting, which may be then transferred to a writing activity. With good initial instruction, children can start to appraise each other's performances, making suggestions about better choices in terms of the language used, the structure of the spoken piece as a whole and the actual delivery. Children should be taught to listen for the use of expression and inflection, which both help to maintain the listener's interest. They can explore the pragmatics, as introduced in Chapter 1 of this book, considering how language varies in different situations and how the actual delivery of the spoken word is changed to suit the circumstances and the intention of what is being said. They can be asked to create recordings which demonstrate different moods in the speaker and even to create ones which are monotonal, to get a feel for the impact (or rather lack of impact) of weak presentation of the spoken word.

Case study   Developing expression

Gabi, a teacher of a Year 4 class in an inner-city school with a high and increasing population of children with English as an additional language, had noticed that when children read aloud from their reading books, there was a lack of expression being used, particularly within the descriptive passages. She had used modelling to highlight and explore this when she read aloud to the class and had encouraged more expressive reading with individuals and with guided groups, but wanted to do an activity which had a very clear focus on developing expressive aspects of reading, beyond those used in dialogue, which the children appeared more able with.

In order to develop more expression in reading, Gabi gave the children a detailed picture of a story setting, the Snow Queen's Palace. She wanted the children to write a detailed description of the palace, building on earlier work on settings and the use of adjectives. The children worked together in small groups, using the picture as a stimulus, to create long descriptive passages.

Gabi then told the class to imagine that this description was going to be part of an audiobook and they were going to work in teams to create a recording of their passage. She shared an example of a description from another audiobook to show what a good one would sound like. The children were given instructions on how to use a simple recording app on an iPad. In turns, each child read the passage and it was then played back. The children were given guidance and a modelled

(Continued)

(Continued)

activity, which showed the potential impact of good or poor clarity, pace, intonation, emphasis and variation in volume when reading. After each recording, the children listened back to it, pausing the recording whenever necessary. The children scored each other for each element and made constructive comments about how to improve the performance. Each child then did second or third takes, improving each time.

The impact of the peer evaluation was immediate and very positive. The recordings showed improvement in the expressive reading for each child and the supportive and constructive comments led to clear changes, which enhanced the reading. The children gained confidence in reading aloud and could hear the differences in their own performances. Later work on creating advertisements showed the impact was sustained over time.

Audio drama

The National Curriculum in England states that children should 'rehearse, refine, share and respond thoughtfully to drama and theatre performances' (DfE, 2013: 14). Engaging children in creating audio drama is another good way to encourage them to explore the use and variety of speech. For Years 3/4, in the National Curriculum, children are expected to prepare *poems and play scripts to read aloud and to perform, showing understanding through intonation, tone, volume and action* (DfE, 2013: 36) and for Years 5/6 to do the same, but replacing 'action' with the additional expectation that *the meaning is clear to an audience* (DfE, 2013: 44). Reading aloud does not always have to be in front of others. Children can create recordings in the style of radio plays or audio recordings of their own presentation of a learned poem.

A stage further could be performance poetry, where the poem is not simply read, but is made into a performance, with significant attention given to the delivery of the words and the potential to use video, so non-verbal communication can be added. There are many examples of children's poets performing their own poems available online. Michael Rosen, for example, has many of his performances available to view (www.michael-rosen.co.uk). These give real contexts for performance and the chance to see good practice in oral presentation being modelled.

Discussion and debate

The National Curriculum requirements for children to *understand and use the conventions for discussion and debate* (DfE 2013: 14) offer opportunities for children to engage in synchronous and asynchronous communication with other participants across the country and the world, through the use of video conferencing, as one synchronous example, or through an online oral discussion application such as Voicethread (voicethread.com), as an asynchronous example.

Presentations

Primary age children are expected to 'make formal presentations' (DfE, 2013: 13) and digital approaches to this requirement are not only possible, but will engage children in the growing phenomenon of personal video publication, epitomised by YouTube.

Schools have often used a 'show and tell' activity with children from very young ages. Children also experience 'presentations' from very young ages, from their teachers and from visitors, for example in school assemblies. For most children in Key Stage 1, with suitable tuition and simple software, the creation of multimedia presentations will not be beyond their ability. If all this is put together, then from a young age children could practise their presentational speaking using digital presentations to support, structure and share what they are saying. In doing this, children will need to focus on the range of presentational skills covered in Chapter 3 and also increasingly on the skills in video and audio editing required to ensure this form of communication is engaging for its intended audience. An anonymised upload to YouTube is possible, but parental permission will be required to allow this. School VLEs may include the facility to upload video, just for the school community to watch, although even this should be supported by parental permission.

Conversation

The use of audio or video calls, whether they are between individuals or as part of groups, is a dimension of education which offers real opportunities for developing skills in dialogue in real-world situations. It is now easier and cheaper than ever before for a whole class to engage in an online, real-time discussion with somebody on the other side of the world. Links between schools in geographically distant places present obvious cross-curricular possibilities, but in terms of developing skills in speaking and listening, the chance to engage in conversation, discussion and debate with a wider range of participants is something which should be capitalised on.

Asynchronous communication, where messages are left to be listened to at a later date, while not perhaps as broadly engaging as the use of real-time audio or video conferencing, can still have a place in the classroom.

Two examples of this are podcasting and using an audio discussion board, such as Voicethread (voicethread.com).

Verbal communication is supported by non-verbal communication and this is where audio-only conversations and information giving can be seen as less effective than face-to-face communication. Telephone conversations, of the standard form, along with things like audio-only podcasts, do not include the additional information gained by a listener who can see the speaker's face, watch the changes in expression and observe the body language, hand gestures and head movements. However, taking away the non-verbal element also has the effect of making the spoken voice far more important to both the listener and the speaker. Children engaged in activities where only the voice is used to communicate can be encouraged to consider tone, volume, stress, emphasis, phrasing, speed, clarity and other factors in what they say and what they hear, building their understanding of the nuances in spoken language. The ability to record and edit what children say is very helpful here.

Video

It is very likely, given the extraordinary growth in children either owning or having access to relatively cheap technology which allows them to access the internet, that when children use the web to find out about a topic which interests them, a video or audio source will be found. An example of this is the plethora of videos available about the computer game *Minecraft*, which is a favourite of many primary-aged children. This is the modern equivalent of hobby magazines, but the huge difference is that this is all based on Web 2.0 technology, meaning anybody with a suitable device can create and distribute videos, as well as comment on them. As a growing aspect of modern communication, personal video creation should be explored in the curriculum.

A simple suggested use for video and a starting point perhaps for children, from Barber and Cooper (2012), is to create or source commentary-free video clips, to which the children have to add speech. An example is for a calculation method in maths, for which the children then have to create a commentary. This method is a clear way of checking understanding, but also provides another format for creating and rehearsing instructional talk. It also offers the opportunity for children to use video and audio editing software to add their own audio commentary to a clip. With software such as Audacity (audacityteam.org) and some training, this is not a task that is beyond primary children, who may even have experienced doing this kind of thing at home with family digital photos and videos. Devices such as iPads have built-in or available apps that can be used. A simpler approach could be to create the commentary and play it back using a device such as an Easi-Speak MP3 Recorder/Player. This is a USB-based microphone record-ing device, which records, plays and stores sound files. Similar activities could be undertaken for other curriculum areas, for example the rain cycle, a historical event or even narrating a story based on a series of pictures or a video. There are many video clips which would be ideal for the last of those activities found on The Literacy Shed website (www.literacyshed.com).

Video also provides a useful tool to help explore non-verbal communication, whether it is a previously recorded video used to consider how things like body language and gesture are used to communicate or videos created by the children to demonstrate and evaluate their own non-verbal communication.

Oral rehearsal

The National Curriculum recognises the value of talk for writing in a variety of forms. One National Curriculum requirement is for children to 'draft and write by: composing and rehearsing sentences orally (including dialogue)' (DfE, 2013: 39). This requirement is based on the impact of oral rehearsal on the quality of writing.

Oral rehearsal (explored in Chapter 5), as part of the writing process, is a useful step to help children craft their compositions as well as they can. Digital devices offer the chance for children to record and review that oral rehearsal in a variety of ways, including: simply recording their own thoughts; recording and playing back a group discussion about what will be written and drama activities where the content of the text to be written out is acted out as fully as possible. In all of these instances, the digital recording provides support for recall of ideas, as illustrated in the following case study.

Case study   Talking tin lids

Sandeep, a teacher working with a Year 1 class in an inner-city primary school, made use of a simple recording and playback device to encour-age children to orally rehearse their sentences prior to writing them, as part of the drafting process. His initial reason for introducing this was to support a small number of children who were orally confident and creative when it came to composition, but whose physical writing skills were still relatively weak, meaning it took a lot of time and effort to transfer the ideas in their heads to the written word on paper. This led to a loss of fluency and growing frustration with writing, as the children

(Continued)

(Continued)

were focused so much on the physical activity of writing that the good word choices and sentences structures were not always transferred well.

The device Sandeep introduced was the talking tin lid. These are products to aid blind or partially sighted people and are designed to fit on top of tins – a simple record/play function allows somebody to record a short message to be played back. In their use as tin lids, this enables sight-impaired people to hear what the content of a tin is. These are cheap digital recording devices and Sandeep's school invested in small sets for each class, to support speaking, listening and writing development. Once the tin lids started to be used by the children to record their sentences before writing them, Sandeep noticed improved written outcomes, particularly for those children whose confidence in their composition was stifled by poor physical writing skills.

This case study shows how even a simple device can be used to enhance children's learning and support the development of effective communication skills.

Final thoughts...

Given the prevalence of digital forms of communication, development of the skills to use technology effectively to communicate, and also using technology to support learning across the English curriculum and beyond, must be essential parts of the approach of all primary teachers. As Papert (the creator of Logo, a well-known early programming language for children) and Markowsky note, 'the explosion of technology has the potential to make education more available and influential than ever before' and we 'must rethink the foundations of education so it can truly benefit from new technology' (Papert and Markowsky, 2013: 31). Rethinking teaching communication skills for the digital age is a key part of that.

References

Barber, D. and Cooper, L. (2012) *Using New Web Tools in the Primary Classroom.* London: Routledge.

Broadbent, H., Fell, L., Green, P. and Gardner, W. (2013) *Have your Say: Listening to young people about their online rights and responsibilities.* Plymouth: Childnet

International and UK Safer Internet Centre. Retrieved from: www.saferinternet.org. uk/research

DCSF (2008) *Safer Children in a Digital World: The Report of the Byron Review.* Nottingham: DCSF Publications.

DfE (2013) *The National Curriculum in England: Key Stages 1 and 2 Framework Document.* London: DfE.

DfEE/QCA (1999) *The National Curriculum: Handbook for primary teachers in England.* London: DfEE/QCA.

Holloway, D., Green, L. and Livingstone, S. (2013) *Zero to Eight. Young children and their internet use.* London: EU Kids Online.

Medwell, J. and Wray, D. (2008) Handwriting – a forgotten language skill? *Language and Education,* 22(1): 34–47.

Ofcom (2014) *Children and Parents: Media Use and Attitudes Report.* Available at: http://stakeholders.ofcom.org.uk/binaries/research/media-literacy/media-use-attitudes-14/Childrens_2014_Report.pdf

Papert, S. and Markowsky, G. (2013) The state of learning: a preview. *Learning Landscapes: Teaching and Learning in the Digital World: Possibilities and Challenges,* 6(2): 31–6.

Plester, B., Wood, C. and Joshi, P. (2009) Exploring the relationship between children's knowledge of text message abbreviations and school literacy outcomes. *British Journal of Developmental Psychology,* 27, 145-161.

Puentedura, R.R. (2013) *The SAMR Model Explained by Ruben R. Puentedura.* Video. Available at: www.youtube.com/watch?v=_QOsz4AaZ2k.

CONCLUSION

We hope that reading this book has helped you consider the value of developing a range of language and communication possibilities in your classroom. We hope, too, that you will make use of the many recommendations for wider reading and links to useful websites to broaden your knowledge and understanding. There is a wealth of material available, most of which can be acquired for little or no cost.

If this book has prompted you to reflect upon your practice as a teacher, and to consider how you can make your classroom into a place where children share ideas confidently, and communicate effectively, then it has been worthwhile.

Kate Allott
David Waugh
March 2016

INDEX